AT
JESUS'
FEET

To order additional copies of *At Jesus' Feet,*
by Doug Batchelor,
call 1-800-765-6955.
Visit us at *www.reviewandherald.com* for information on other
Review and Herald products.

THE GOSPEL ACCORDING TO
MARY MAGDALENE

AT JESUS' FEET

DOUG BATCHELOR

REVIEW AND HERALD ® PUBLISHING ASSOCIATION
HAGERSTOWN, MD 21740

The author assumes full responsibility for the accuracy of all facts and
quotations as cited in this book.

Unless otherwise noted, all Scripture references are from the New King James
Version. Copyright © 1979, 1980, 1982 by Thomas Nelson, Inc. Used by permission.
All rights reserved.

Scripture quotations marked NASB are from the *New American Standard Bible,* ©
The Lockman Foundation 1960, 1962, 1963, 1968, 1971, 1972, 1973, 1975, 1977.

Bible texts credited to NRSV are from the New Revised Standard Version of the
Bible, copyright © 1989 by the Division of Christian Education of the National Council
of the Churches of Christ in the U.S.A. Used by permission.

This book was
Edited by Raymond H. Woolsey
Copyedited by Delma Miller
Cover photo by Don Satterlee
Designed by Tina Ivany
Electronic makeup by Shirley M. Bolivar
Typeset: 12/14 Bembo

PRINTED IN U.S.A.
04 03 02 01 00   5 4 3 2 1

R&H Cataloging Service
Batchelor, Doug, 1957-
    At Jesus' feet: the gospel according to Mary Magdalene.

    1. Jesus Christ.   2. Salvation.   3. Mary Magdalene.
I. Title.

                    232.954

ISBN 0-8280-1589-9, hardcover
ISBN 0-8280-1590-2, paperback

THANKS TO . . .

Writing is a jealous mistress that demands undivided attention. Every line in this book represents a sacrifice laid on the altar of time made by my loving wife, Karen. I thank her for her support, patience, and encouragement as I tried to carve out precious hours to complete this work.

Thanks to Bonnie, a better secretary than anyone deserves.

In order to bring the story of Mary alive, in this book I dared to venture into a new realm of marrying biblical facts with plausible fiction, and then encapsulate it within an expository study. Because for me this was uncharted territory, I turned to Kay Rizzo for seasoned experience with editing and some creative input. Many thanks!

CONTENTS

PREFACE

Why a book about Mary Magdalene? Was she a great intellect like Solomon? Probably not. As beautiful as Bathsheba? The Bible is silent on this point. She was generous with her means, but she did not possess the wealth of Zacchaeus. When she thought Jesus' body had been evicted from Joseph's tomb, Mary boldly offered to carry away the Carpenter's remains. Did that imply she was physically strong, a female Samson?

Her fame doesn't come from the coveted traits the world typically associates with greatness. So what makes Mary special? This woman demonstrated three traits worthy of merit: a great love, a tenacious loyalty, and a perfect devotion. And all this springs from a life that was dirty and broken.

Most of us will never experience the wisdom and riches of Solomon or the beauty of Bathsheba, but if we let Mary teach us, like her we can be clean and new again. We can grow beyond our weaknesses, and we can possess that same tremendous love and devotion to serve Jesus here and through all eternity. With humble steps we too can follow Mary from abject shame to songs of gratitude and praise.

THE STORY AND THE STUDY

I have divided this book into two parts, the story and the study. People will lean closer and strain their ears to hear a good story, but jump and run at the first sign of study.

I chose the subject of Mary Magdalene because her life provides the best of both worlds—a moving story that is also a fascinating and edifying study. The wonderful stories of Mary in Scripture provide the perfect spiritual springboard to profound yet simple studies that will root the reader in the fundamental truths of God's Word.

You may be tempted to just read the stories of Mary and skip over the studies. That would be like coming home from the market after shopping for dinner to discover that you had left the bag with the main course at the checkout counter and brought home only the dessert.

I assure you, most of the study sections also contain some good stories.

—DEB

INTRODUCTION

Writing this book has provided a unique and new challenge for me. In order to weave together the various stories and events in which Mary appears and maintain a connected flow in the areas in which the Bible is silent, I've had to tug on a few fibers of imagination and a strand or two of sanctified supposition. Wherever possible I have faithfully done my best to build upon what is revealed in Scripture and inspired commentaries.

First, let me say that I do not claim to be a prophet or the son of a prophet; however, in the five-year process of writing this manuscript, more than once I have prayed that God would help me see what happened 2,000 years ago so I could be accurate in communicating the events. There were several times when I was staring at my computer screen that I felt as if I were transported back and shown different aspects of Mary's life, as if I were there watching her drama unfold.

I am eagerly looking forward to the day when I meet the characters in this volume so that I can discover if these "visions" were divine revelation or overactive imagination. Perhaps a bit of both? Ultimately I am longing to meet Jesus face-to-face, who saved me, as He did Mary, from the depths of sin.

CHAPTER ONE

ADULTERY IN THE TEMPLE!

The Story

G rab her!" an angry voice shouted, shattering the early-morning silence. The heavy wooden door opened and slammed against the wall with a thud, making a deeper hole in the already-damaged plaster.

Startled by this sudden invasion, Mary's heart froze. It appeared that the day she'd feared most had come.

"Adulterer! Prostitute!" the invaders shouted. Contempt dripped from their leering faces, like saliva from the mouths of rabid dogs. The Temple rabbis and priests poured into her small, private place of business, intent on the kill.

Her customer slipped from beneath her sheets, cast her a sheepish shrug, and drew on his clothing, acting not at all surprised by the intrusion.

This is a trap! she thought as she gazed at the men standing against the wall in the shadows, their embarrassed faces shrouded with the last remnants of night. Several were her former clients, but she knew that to identify them now would only intensify her impending punishment.

From time to time, in order to maintain a semblance of piety and to appease the devout among the people, the scribes, lawyers, and priests would make an example of one of the out-of-town prostitutes by parading her through the streets for the gawking bystanders to curse and spit on. Then, in a mockery of pious zeal, they would violently expel their victim from the holy city through the Dung Gate in a display of artificial indignation.

I should have stayed in Magdala, Mary thought as she clutched the flimsy bedsheet. Gathering the bedding about her to hide her nakedness, she struggled to her feet.

"Seize her! Don't let her get away," one of the priests snarled while another lunged for her. A third person, a Temple guard, grabbed her by her upper arm, his nails digging into her tender flesh.

Mary tried to resist, but the man's grip held fast. The terrified woman began to tremble uncontrollably. She had been suspicious when this new customer appeared at the door of her room so early in the morning. *They're going to make an example of me*

"Get her some clothes." One of the lawyers snatched her from the guard's clutches.

"Humph! I say take her as she is," a scribe defended. "It will be more convincing."

"No, He is in the Temple, and we can't take her to the Temple like that!" an older priest added with final authority as he ran his eyes over her quivering body.

One of the men leaning against the wall handed the priest a crumpled and dirty robe that had been draped over a small stool.

"Put this on. Hide your shame!" the priest snapped, tossing the soiled garment at the quaking woman. Grateful for even the crude covering, Mary snatched the robe from the man's outstretched hand and wrapped it about herself. Though a prostitute, she still had a sense of modesty. Under the gaze of the lusting eyes of her accusers she covered her naked body. Her fingers trembled as she tied the belt of the dirty, oversized robe about her waist.

Upon command of the older priest, the two Temple guards seized her arms and pulled her toward the door. The rabbis stepped back, allowing the guards and the woman to pass. She exchanged a knowing glance with one of the rabbis. He lowered his eyes in shame. Revered leaders of his stature would never touch a woman with her reputation—in public, that is.

The guards dragged her through the streets. Their muscular fingers bruised her olive skin. Her long, splendid hair, her pride and glory, fell tangled over her face. She struggled to maintain her footing over the rocks along the roadway. *Where are they taking me?* she wondered. Up ahead loomed the holy Temple. *The Temple?* Her panic grew. *Why the Temple?*

She could hear the shouts and curses from spectators as they passed. Curious housewives and merchants began to fall in behind this strange procession.

O God, Mary prayed desperately, *please don't let Martha and Lazarus see me as I really am.* A sick, hopeless laugh burst through her sobs. *How can I expect the pure Holy One of Israel to hear the prayer of a filthy sinner such as I? I've gone so far, too far for God ever to forgive or hear my prayers.*

A movement off to the side of the narrow street caused Mary's breath to catch in her throat. Priests were picking up some of the large stones that were intermittently scattered in front of the buildings, used to hold open the shop doors.

"They are going to stone me!" she gasped. A small pack of agitated dogs followed the procession up the street, yapping at the unusual early-morning excitement. Mary wailed. "They're going to stone me to death, and then those scavenging dogs will eat me as they did Jezebel!"

She'd heard the story many times, growing up in a faithful Jewish home. But she'd never imagined her fate would be the same as that of Ahab's wicked queen. The guard holding her right arm gave her a brief look of sympathy, then redirected his attention to plowing through the growing sea of nosy spectators. On her left she saw a shop-keeper pick up a rock. A fish salesman on her right did the same. Mary's mind raced. Her trembling increased. Her breath came in short gasps. Spots danced before her eyes; she felt as if she were in a tunnel and thought she might faint.

"Why are they taking me to the Temple?" Mary asked the guard who held her right arm, her eyes filled with perplexity and pain. "Why don't they stone me outside the gate?"

The guard whispered out of the side of his mouth into the pretty young woman's ear: "You may still have a chance. If they stone the Teacher, they will probably let you go. He's the one they want."

The Teacher! She had heard about the Teacher who went about the country healing people and blessing them. Everyone had heard

of the Teacher. Soon she saw, above the crowd of curious spectators, feast worshipers, and swirling dust, the white walls of God's
sanctuary, gleaming golden in the early-morning sunlight.

A cool breeze riffled her long brown hair. Mary shivered. The
woman wasn't sure which frightened her more, the thought she might
soon be stoned to death for adultery or that she was being paraded into
the house of God half-naked and guilty of a scandalous crime.

With brute force the priests and guards pressed through the last
100 feet leading into the courtyard, where an assembly of angry
money changers and sacrifice merchants clustered at the entrance to
the Temple. *That's strange,* Mary thought. *They usually bring their animals and money tables into the courtyard.*

Several agitated sacrifice salesmen accosted the priests who were
accompanying Mary. "He made a whip and chased us out," one
snarled. "He knocked over my money table!"

"Who gave this Galilean such authority?" asked another, shaking
his fist in the rabbi's face. "This Man must be stopped!"

With renewed determination the priests stooped their necks and
headed into the Temple. Caught up in the developing drama, Mary
had almost forgotten her part until an angry young woman pulled
aside her veil and screeched in Mary's face. "Harlot!" the woman
barked. Then, like a camel, she hurled a well-aimed missile of saliva
in Mary's direction, striking her robe. Mary looked down at the
blotch on her already soiled garment and cringed. She'd never felt
so dirty.

Inside the sacred courtyard the atmosphere drastically changed.
The familiar bleating of the goats and sheep, the cooing of the
quail, and all the barnyard smells that a worshiper usually encoun-
tered upon entering the Temple courtyard were missing. Instead
there was a sweet air of peace and silent awe. Without warning, the
guards slowed their pace, then stopped. They loosened their iron
grip on her upper arms. She rubbed her bruised skin.

The priests leading the procession had halted as well. In muffled
tones they discussed the surprising turn of events, then straightened
to regain their arrogant, pious composure. "There! There He is,"
one of them whispered. He pointed to a large crowd gathered

around Someone sitting on the Temple steps.

The priests paused to shake the dust from the bottom of their robes and folded their hands together within the blue tasseled sleeves of their fine white garments to assume a respectable religious demeanor. Then, exchanging a smug and sinister nod at each other, they strode across the marble hall to the cluster of worshipers assembled on the steps. The Temple guards, less hostile toward the woman in their charge, followed.

As the priestly procession moved toward the heart of the crowd, the worshipers parted for them to pass, until they stood before the One who was obviously the center of the gathering.

Mary stared in awe. Although she had heard of Him—everyone had—she had never seen a man like this before. His features were angular, rugged, obviously not a stranger to hard work or outdoor living. Yet in His countenance she saw a gentleness, an expression of innocence mixed with wisdom and dignity. His whole frame had a perfect symmetry and balance that bore a combination of nobility and compassion. Mary had never before seen such majesty in any man, and Mary had known many men.

For some strange reason she couldn't identify, Mary felt a sense of peace and safety in His presence. Surrounded by a wall of onlookers making an escape impossible, the guards released their grip on Mary, and she collapsed, trembling, at Jesus' feet.

Mary closed her eyes and folded her arms over her head, unable to continue gazing upon this holy Man, wishing she could make this nightmare disappear. Above the din of shouts and mocking, she heard her accusers present before Jesus their lethal charge against her. "Teacher, this woman was caught in adultery, in the very act. Now Moses, in the law, commanded us that such should be stoned. But what do You say?" (John 8:4, 5).

The reality of her hopeless and mortifying situation crushed Mary. The terrifying array of emotions caused her to lose consciousness briefly. Crumpled on the cold marble pavement as she was, no one even knew she fainted—no one except Jesus, who'd missed nothing about the young woman. Long before she'd entered the courtyard, long before she'd taken the first stranger to her bed, long before she'd taken the first step that would lead to her mortification, He had anticipated this very instant in time.

After a few moments Mary regained consciousness. The courtyard atmosphere had changed. It was strangely quiet. She peeked out from under her disheveled hair to see Jesus calmly tracing words in the dust of the Temple floor. At first she couldn't make out the words. She watched as He stood and said, "He who is without sin among you, let him throw a stone at her first" (verse 7).

She cringed, expecting a hail of stones to descend upon her. Instead she heard a thud and someone walking away.

Opening her eyes, she watched as the Teacher stooped down once more and continued writing. What was He writing? She listened to the whispers of the diminishing crowd. He was enumerating the sins of the Temple officials for all to see.

After what seemed like an eternity, the gentle hand of Jesus touched her shoulder. She brushed her hair from her face and raised her eyes. Mary saw Jesus looking back at her with infinite compassion. On His face was a slightly quizzical smile, as if He were wondering why she would be groveling in such an undignified manor in this holy place. Standing slowly, she gazed about and saw that the scribes and Pharisees were gone. The hypocrites who had entrapped her had fled the Temple. Then Jesus addressed her with a term of respect, "Madam, where are your accusers? Has no one condemned you?" (see verse 10).

Mary looked around bewildered and said, "No one, Lord" (verse 11).

And Jesus said to her, "Neither do I condemn you; go and sin no more" (verse 11).

Mary thought this was too good to be true. *"Go and don't do it again"? I'm an adulterer! And His only rebuke is "Go and sin no more"?*

Could it be true that she was free to go? She'd been reprieved, rescued from her just punishment. Her initial instinct was to flee the place as quickly as possible, but she felt constrained by an overwhelming gratitude to thank her advocate. Willingly Mary threw herself at the Master's feet and poured out her heartfelt appreciation mingled with tears. As she did, she looked at the ground and saw the word "adulterer" staring back at her. Her face flamed at the polished, bright letters, a vivid, stark relief against the dust on the marble floor.

Before she could seek answers in the face of the gentle Teacher, a strong morning breeze came through the Temple court, erasing the entire catalog of sins etched in the dust. At that moment Mary felt an enormous burden of guilt lift from her soul.

The Study

JOHN 8:2-11

"Now early in the morning He came again into the temple, and all the people came to Him; and He sat down and taught them. Then the scribes and Pharisees brought to Him a woman caught in adultery. And when they had set her in the midst, they said to Him, 'Teacher, this woman was caught in adultery, in the very act. Now Moses, in the law, commanded us that such should be stoned. But what do You say?'

"This they said, testing Him, that they might have something of which to accuse Him. But Jesus stooped down and wrote on the ground with His finger, as though He did not hear. So when they continued asking Him, He raised Himself up and said to them, 'He who is without sin among you, let him throw a stone at her first.'

"And again He stooped down and wrote on the ground. Then those who heard it, being convicted by their conscience, went out one by one, beginning with the oldest even to the last. And Jesus was left alone, and the woman standing in the midst. When Jesus had raised Himself up and saw no one but the woman, He said to her, 'Woman, where are those accusers of yours? Has no one condemned you?' She said, 'No one, Lord.' And Jesus said to her, 'Neither do I condemn you; go and sin no more.'

WHO WAS MARY?

Who was this woman caught in adultery? The Bible never identifies her by name, but I believe that this was Mary Magdalene and that this story, found only in the Gospel of John, was Jesus' first encounter with her. Here she is simply referred to as "a woman." But in other places in the Gospel stories Mary is also called "a woman" (Luke 7:37). Perhaps this is because, after this experience, Mary became a very devoted disciple, and John, recognizing this to be an extremely embarrassing situation, chose to tell her story in a more anonymous format to protect her reputation.

For the following reasons I, along with many New Testament scholars, believe that Mary Magdalene and the Mary of Bethany mentioned in the Gospels are the same Mary. Here are a few reasons:

1. Neither was married.
2. Both had bad reputations.
3. Both had money.
4. Both had the same name.
5. Both were with Jesus, but their names are never mentioned together.

Texts that help verify this view include:

1. "Now after the Sabbath, as the first day of the week began to dawn, Mary Magdalene and the other Mary came to see the tomb" (Matt. 28:1). The "other Mary" is understood to be the mother of James and Joses, and the wife of Clopas.

2. "Is this not the carpenter, the Son of Mary, and brother of James, Joses, Judas, and Simon? And are not His sisters here with us?" (Mark 6:3).

3. "Among whom were Mary Magdalene, Mary the mother of James and Joses, and the mother of Zebedee's sons" (Matt. 27:56).

4. "There were also women looking on from afar, among whom were Mary Magdalene, Mary the mother of James the Less and of Joses, and Salome" (Mark 15:40).

The name Mary is the Greek equivalent of the Hebrew *Miriam,* meaning "bitter." And in our first introduction to Mary, we find her in bitter shame. But here is the bigger question: How did the name Mary Magdalene come to take on such a connotation of immorality? How does a woman get to the place where she will auction herself nightly to the highest bidder? A desperate need for funds can drive a mother to prostitution in order to provide for her children, but in most cases, the cause is something deeper.

Looking for love

Several years ago I had a job in Palm Springs, California, playing the guitar and flute in an after-hours hippie restaurant called The Peach and Frog. The job didn't last very long because the manager could see I was not a very good musician and was an even poorer vocalist. However, most of the patrons came in half drunk after the other bars in town had closed, and they thought I sounded just fine.

One night (or perhaps I should say early morning) during my short career as a folk singer I got off work about 3:00 a.m. and began driving my Volkswagon up the deserted street to my apartment. On the main drag in Palm Springs I noticed a man about 55 and his 20-year-old daughter sitting at a bus stop.

They must be tourists, I thought, *and don't know that the buses stop running after midnight.* I was a new Christian and had much to learn. Wanting to be a good Samaritan, I pulled over and told them the buses weren't running at this hour.

The inebriated man gazed at me through blurred eyes and slurred, "We called a cab an hour ago, and it never came." I had no doubt that he had been drinking more than a little.

"Well, how far are you going?" I asked.

"To the hotel two miles down toward the south end of town," he said with a hopeful note in his voice.

"OK, hop in, and I'll take you there."

Both the man and the girl chose to squeeze into the back of my VW Bug rather than one sitting in the more spacious front seat.

As I drove the short distance to the hotel I occasionally glanced into the rearview mirror at my two passengers and surmised that this was not a father-daughter relationship after all.

When I eased my car to a stop in front of the hotel, the older man kissed the young woman farewell, struggled out of my under-sized back seat, and stumbled away, calling "Thanks" over his shoulder. I wasn't sure whom he was thanking.

I sat there for a moment in confused awkward silence, then regained enough presence to ask my remaining passenger, "And where are you going?"

"I live in the north end of town," she responded sheepishly.

Calmly I spun my VW around and headed back in the direction from which I had just come. Again I glanced in the rearview mirror and could see from the streetlights occasionally illuminating her young face that she wore an empty, hollow, faraway expression. She looked like exhibit number 1 for unhappiness!

I wanted to help. I had recently been introduced to Jesus through the Scriptures and was eager to tell everyone about the peace that I had found when I asked Him to take control of my messed-up life.

"Would you like to stop and get a cup of coffee?" I asked, trying to sound nonchalant and friendly.

"Sure, why not?" she said, looking back at me in the mirror, her eyes sizing me up for the first time.

In time I learned that this is not the best method for witnessing. But I was a young, impulsive, baby Christian. I didn't know any better at the time, and I am sure that my loving Father winked at my ignorance (Acts 17:30). Today I would advise young men to avoid potential problems by not giving Bible studies to lone young women, especially at 3:30 in the morning.

I pulled into an all-night coffee shop. We had no trouble finding a seat at that hour of the morning. After a few minutes of small talk I learned her name, Marlene. And I asked, "So . . . you a hooker?" I've always been a little abrupt.

She seemed only slightly surprised at my question and responded with a nod and a wily smile that seemed to say, "Open for business."

When I realized my intentions had been misunderstood, I was startled and more than a little embarrassed. I quickly asked, "Are you happy?"

Now it was her turn to be surprised. Her whole demeanor changed. It was as though my question had brought her back to the reality of her miserable condition and the tremendous guilt and shame weighing on her soul.

When she didn't reply, I told her how messed up and empty my life had been until I met the Lord. In turn, Marlene related how she had run away from a loveless home and now was living with some ruthless pimp who beat her one day and bought her little trinkets the next, spending all the money she brought home for himself. Tears welled up in her eyes, then spilled down her cheeks, forming little canyons in her thick mascara. Marlene was 17 years old.

We talked for about an hour. I gave her suggestions on how she could get started in a new life. When I then drove her home I had prayer with her.

I don't remember most of our conversation that night, but one thing I will never forget is her plea, "I just want someone to love me!"

I wonder how many women and men around the world are in trouble because of the same misguided attempts to fill the vacuum in their hearts, not with God's love, but with some cheap substitute. As the country song goes, they're "looking for love in all the wrong places."

ADDICTED TO GOD

I have a radical theory that God made all humans to be addicts. That's right, every one of us is an addict, and God designed us that way! That is, God wired us to be addicted to Him. And when people reject Him, they struggle in vain to fill that cavernous black hole with some other obsession.

Some become workaholics; some become addicted to food and suffer bulimia or obesity. Others choose alcohol, drugs, or cigarettes as their favorite addiction. For some, it's sex or music; still others, fashion and outward appearances. They become consumed with materialism and vanity. And there are those who become addicted to other people in twisted codependent relationships. All this is done in a misguided attempt to fill a void designed for God.

Human beings were created to be filled with God's Spirit, and when God is not the center of their lives they will desperately seek to fill that vacuum with something else. God designed us to be addicted in love to Him. It is only in Him that we will find joy and satisfaction.

BACK TO THE STORY

Let's take a closer look at what was happening with Mary in the Temple that day. The Jewish leaders wanted to destroy Jesus and were willing to embarrass or even execute a misguided young woman in order to accomplish their means. Today we would call this entrapment.

The early hour of this event suggests it was a setup, and obviously " it takes two to tango." What happened to the man involved? If it was a setup, the man very well may have joined the crowd, holding a bag of rocks, ready to stone her at a moment's notice.

That is just like the devil. He entices us to sin, then stands by to accuse and condemn. The father of lies will tell you to do something wrong and then turn you in for listening to him.

None of this came as a surprise for the divine Teacher. In one brief glance Jesus took in the whole scene. He read the proud, conniving motives of the leaders. And He recognized the brokenhearted humiliation of the trembling and weeping woman at His feet.

In His wisdom and love, Jesus would not increase her shame by directing His gaze toward her. The One who will someday judge the world could have burned her to smoldering ashes with a glance, but He came not to condemn, but to save (John 3:17).

The scribes and Pharisees pressed their case: " 'Now Moses, in the law, commanded us that such should be stoned. But what do You say?' This they said, testing Him, that they might have something of which to accuse Him. But Jesus stooped down and wrote on the ground with His finger, as though He did not hear" (John 8:5, 6).

These pompous religious leaders believed their sinister plot to be flawless. If Jesus agreed with the Law of Moses, they planned to immediately drag Mary out of the city and stone her to death. They would then dash to the Romans and report that Jesus had assumed an authority reserved only for the Roman government, the power to pronounce the death penalty. (This was why they would later bring Jesus to Pilate, in order to secure the execution order to crucify Him.)

On the other hand, if Jesus said "Let her go," He would be walking into yet another pit of vipers. The scribes and Pharisees knew that, since the Romans had occupied Palestine and forced their pagan culture on Israel, the people had developed a zealous, jealous devotion for Moses and the Law. The religious leaders planned to feign indignation and incite a riot among the people. They would stone Jesus as being anti-Moses. (A few years later they would try the same thing with the apostle Paul, as noted in Acts 21:28.) Either way Jesus responded, they expected to have themselves a stoning that morning.

Jesus didn't give these hypocrites a glance of recognition. Instead

He stooped down and wrote with His finger in the dust on the Temple floor. He would encourage Mary and humble the scribes and Pharisees.

"You will save the humble people; but Your eyes are on the haughty, that You may bring them down" (2 Sam. 22:28).

The scribes and Pharisees were outraged that Jesus dared to challenge, ignore, and even assume their authority. A few hours earlier He had chased the money changers out of the Temple; the merchants still cowered at the gate, fearing the authority of Jesus and simmering over their undignified retreat.

Yes, the religious leaders were confident that their trap was foolproof, but it was essential that He respond one way or the other. So they repeated their question and pressed for a reply. They never anticipated the answer Jesus gave them.

JUDGMENT

"So when they continued asking Him, He raised Himself up and said to them, 'He who is without sin among you, let him throw a stone at her first.' And again He stooped down and wrote on the ground" (John 8:7, 8).

When they heard this, their mouths fell open. They turned to one another, wondering how to combat this unexpected response. The growing crowd of spectators and worshipers turned their penetrating gazes onto the religious leaders. Would any of these corrupt Temple officials dare to throw the first stone and thereby claim to be sinless? Even the Old Testament scriptures stated that all men had sinned.

"For there is no one who does not sin" (1 Kings 8:46).

"All we like sheep have gone astray; we have turned, every one, to his own way" (Isa. 53:6).

"There is none who does good, no, not one" (Ps. 14:3).

While they frantically sought an appropriate rebuttal to this Man's piercing invitation, they looked down and noticed, for the first time, what Jesus was writing in the dust on the marble pavement.

Three times in the Bible it is recorded that God wrote something:

1. He wrote the Ten Commandments in stone with His finger.

2. He wrote the judgment of Babylon with His finger on the walls of her banquet hall.

3. And He wrote out the sins of the hypocrites with His finger, in the dust of the Temple floor.

At times we have all played the part of hypocrites. But good news! Although Jesus carved the law in eternal stone and etched Babylon's curse on cedar walls, He writes our sins in dust—dust that can vanish, erased by the breath of His love and forgiveness!

There, before the eyes of the proud and the haughty, in perfect Hebrew lettering, Jesus revealed their sins. "Pride, greed, lying, evil thoughts, covetousness." Terrifying fear seized their hearts as they suddenly realized they were in the presence of One who could read their whole lives at a glance. The men who outwardly claimed to be God's men but inwardly made deals with the devil now sensed they were standing before the One who would one day judge the world: "The Lord Jesus Christ, who will judge the living and the dead at His appearing and His kingdom" (2 Tim. 4:1).

The tables had turned. Instead of the prostitute being on trial for her sins, they were on trial and found guilty. The blood drained from their faces. Some began to hyperventilate. Some hid their eyes in shame, sensing that their false cloak of self-righteousness had been torn away, exposing their naked hypocrisy to all.

Some instinctively turned to their elders for guidance. The shocked elders were also speechless. They had the longest record of sins. In humiliation they covered their haughty heads and fled from the presence of Jesus and from the sacred Temple courts.

The book of Revelation tells us that this scene will be repeated when Jesus returns from heaven for the faithful. The wicked and the haughty will flee from His presence and say "to the mountains and rocks, 'Fall on us and hide us from the face of Him who sits on the throne and from the wrath of the Lamb!'" (Rev. 6:16).

"Then those who heard it, being convicted by their conscience, went out one by one, beginning with the oldest even to the last" (John 8:9).

Like cockroaches scurrying for dark corners when the lights come on, Mary's accusers fled from the Master's holy presence. The

Bible tells us that there is an aspect of judgment that takes place just before Jesus comes back, because when He returns He will dish out life and death rewards: "And behold, I am coming quickly, and My reward is with Me, to give to every one according to his work" (Rev. 22:12).

So, obviously, some aspect of judgment takes place *before* Jesus comes. The apostle Peter tells us the focus of this judgment on professed believers. Those who say "Lord, Lord" but do not do His will, will be exposed. "For the time has come for judgment to begin at the house of God; and if it begins with us first, what will be the end of those who do not obey the gospel of God?" (1 Peter 4:17).

Just as the judgment of Mary took place in the Temple, this judgment begins with the elders: "So they began with the elders who were before the temple" (Eze. 9:6).

STONE-THROWING

In Scripture a pure and chaste woman symbolizes the church: "I have likened the daughter of Zion to a lovely and delicate woman" (Jer. 6:2); "Husbands, love your wives, just as Christ also loved the church" (Eph. 5:25); "The Elder, to the elect lady" (2 John 1).

Throughout the Bible there is a continuing parallel between Mary and the church. In Revelation 12 the devil is trying to destroy a woman of light who is a symbol of God's church. And like the false religious leaders in Mary's story, Satan stands by while they accuse the woman: "For the accuser of our brethren, who accused them before our God day and night, has been cast down" (verse 10). "Then he showed me the high priest Joshua standing before the angel of the Lord, and Satan standing at his right hand to accuse him" (Zech. 3:1, NRSV).

The spirit of accusation and of stone-throwing is not the spirit of Christ but the spirit of the enemy. Yet for many, criticizing God's church has become second nature and a very popular form of religious recreation, sort of like discussing the weather. Such persons should be wary of speaking ill of the church. In spite of all her imperfections, she is still the "apple of [God's] eye" (Zech. 2:8).

When we sit in the Pharisees' pew, throwing stones at others in judgment and accusation, we may one day witness the finger of Jesus writing our sins in the dust for all to see.

STANDING FOR SENTENCING

"And Jesus was left alone, and the woman standing in the midst. When Jesus had raised Himself up . . . [He] saw no one but the woman" (John 8:9, 10).

At this point in the story Mary is standing face-to-face with Jesus. She awaits His censure.

Around the world it has been the custom for ages that the accused person stand before the judge when sentence is pronounced. "For we shall all stand before the judgment seat of Christ" (Rom. 14:10).

At the end of time, when the Judge of the highest court stands, He is no longer listening to evidence. He is ready to pronounce judgment. When the pre-Advent judgment of the church is complete, Michael (Jesus) will stand up and there will be a great time of trouble; then Jesus will return to this earth (Dan. 12:1, 2).

JUDGMENT AND PERFECTION

Jesus said that He did not come to condemn sinners, but neither did He come to condone sin! As a trembling Mary stood before Him, awaiting her sentencing, I believe she read love and compassion in His face. Though she knew not of the grace He offered, she was believed and received. "Neither do I condemn you," He said.

But lest we misunderstand the deadly nature of sin He added, "Go and sin no more."

Wait, someone is thinking, *is Jesus asking us to be sinless?* Absolutely. Jesus can never say anything less. Sin is the disease that was killing Mary.

What would you have Jesus say? "Go and sin a little less"? "Go and cut back on your life of prostitution"? Jesus did not come to save us *in* our sin but *from* our sin (Matt. 1:21). We are saved from the penalty and from the power, and ultimately the presence, of sin. Personally, I do not claim to be perfect, but I am a follower of a perfect Saviour. And Jesus left me a perfect example.

If I should say that God can't keep me from sinning, I venture onto deadly ground. In essence I say, "The devil is powerful enough to tempt me to sin, but Jesus isn't powerful enough to keep me from sin." Scripture promises, "He who is in you is greater than he who is in the world" (1 John 4:4). If I could manufacture an excuse for sin, it would cease to be sin.

Also, I accuse God of a gross and cruel injustice in asking me to do the impossible, then punishing me for not doing it. That would be something like a father asking his young toddler to touch the ceiling. And as the little one strains on tiptoes to reach up seven feet, vainly jumping with his pudgy legs to gain only an inch or two, the father swings his hand down and smacks the child, sending him sprawling to the ground. "I told you to touch the ceiling and you disobeyed me!"

An ugly picture, to be sure. But suppose I ask my toddler to touch the ceiling, and as he is straining and stretching to do the impossible, I gently reach down and lift him up to his goal. This is how the Bible pictures God. In every command of God the inherent power to obey is available. When the heavenly Father asked His children to cross an ocean without a boat, He parted the sea; in Peter's case, He enabled him to walk on water. In today's vernacular, He might give us scuba gear!

SIN NO LONGER REIGNS

Sin is more than a single offense; sin is an ongoing pattern, a lifestyle. Before Jesus saves us, we are slaves to our sins. After Jesus saves us, we may fall occasionally and bruise our knees, but "sin shall not have dominion over you" (Rom. 6:14).

For the Christian, where sin once sat enthroned and unchallenged Jesus now sits as Lord and King. "Therefore do not let sin reign in your mortal body, that you should obey it in its lusts" (verse 12). This does not mean genuine Christians will not make mistakes. John said, "My little children, these things I write to you, so that you may not sin. And if anyone sins, we have an Advocate with the Father, Jesus Christ the righteous" (1 John 2:1).

This concept is described in greater detail in that famous book *Steps to Christ:* "The character is revealed, not by occasional good deeds and occasional misdeeds, but by the tendency of the habitual words and acts" (pp. 57, 58).

NOT CONDONING OR CONDEMNING

"He said to her, 'Woman, where are those accusers of yours? Has no one condemned you?' She said, 'No one, Lord.' And Jesus said to her, 'Neither do I condemn you; go and sin no more' " (John 8:10, 11).

Wait, she was guilty! Is Jesus condoning adultery here? No, never! Jesus' statement confirms the opposite. The Son of the living God views adultery as a sin when He says, "Go and *sin* no more."

The woman's accusers were gone. The charges were therefore dropped on a technicality. And Jesus already had said that He was not going to accuse her. She was free to go.

Think about it. If Jesus came to accuse us of our sins, there wouldn't be enough rocks in the world to stone the guilty, nor innocents enough to hurl the stones.

"For God did not send His Son into the world to condemn the world, but that the world through Him might be saved" (John 3:17).

If condemnation were His reason for coming to earth, He didn't need to come at all, for we are born condemned. "He who believes in Him is not condemned; but he who does not believe is condemned already, because he has not believed in the name of the only begotten Son of God" (verse 18).

Some suggest that when Jesus told Mary, "Neither do I condemn you" (John 8:11), He was in effect saying that the law had now been set aside. But in fact, the opposite is true! "Sin is the transgression of the law" (1 John 3:4, KJV).

In essence, Jesus was telling Mary, "I will take your penalty because I love you. Sin hurts you, and sin hurts Me. I will be a sacrifice in your place. Because you love Me, go and sin [break the law] no more."

REAL REPENTANCE

Sarah was a wonderful Christian woman who had a rare and deep relationship with her Lord. But her brother George was the proverbial black sheep of the family, the antithesis of the life of his sister. George had a severe alcohol problem. After years of abuse his body re belled. His kidneys were failing fast. The doctors told Sarah that George would surely die soon if he did not receive a kidney transplant.

"So, what about a transplant?" she asked.

"Because of George's history of drinking, it's doubtful that he would even qualify to have his name added to the list of organ recipients." Without hesitation Sarah asked the doctors if she could give one of her kidneys to her ailing brother.

"If your blood types match, you could," the doctor replied. "But this is an expensive operation, and we question the wisdom of putting your health at risk for a person with such self-destructive habits."

"Please, Doctor. Just find out if my kidney is even suitable."

It turned out that their blood types did match. When the accounting department brought up the subject of money—George had no insurance—Sarah mortgaged her home and assumed responsibility to pay whatever was needed. With determined persistence, she persuaded the hospital and the kidney transplant team to perform the surgery.

The transplant procedure went fine—for George, that is, but not for Sarah. Sarah had a rare allergic reaction to the anesthetic, and after the surgery found herself paralyzed from the waist down.

Sarah was able to bear the tragic news a little better when she was told that George was doing remarkably well. "Thank God," she said. "If I am able to buy my brother a few more years of life in which to find the Saviour, then it was still worth it, even if I can never walk again."

How noble and generous of the loving sister. However, her nobility is not the reason I tell this story, for life is stranger than fiction. How do you think Sarah felt when her brother never stopped by her bed to thank her for her costly sacrifice? And how do you think Sarah felt when she learned that the first thing her brother did after leaving the hospital was to go to a bar and celebrate?

Most of the world eagerly takes the blessings of God and selfishly squanders them, as did George. How do you think Jesus feels when a professed Christian, after receiving mercy and life, leaves His presence and returns to the very behavior that cost the Saviour such suffering? When we see and understand how much our sins have cost Him, we will no longer want to embrace the monster that cut Him so deeply.

Jesus didn't die on the cross to buy us a license *to* sin; He came to save us *from* sin. And love is the power that enables us to turn from those sins. "Do you despise the riches of His goodness, forbearance, and longsuffering, not knowing that the goodness of God leads you to repentance?" (Rom. 2:4).

REPEAT OFFENDERS

Mary's story does not end on the Temple floor. Neither do our stories. Because we may repeat the same mistakes and fall into the same sin more than once does not mean that God has forsaken us. "And the twelve were with Him, and certain women who had been healed of evil spirits and infirmities—Mary called Magdalene, out of whom had come seven demons" (Luke 8:2). "Now when He rose early on the first day of the week, He appeared first to Mary Magdalene, out of whom He had cast seven demons" (Mark 16:9). Seven times Mary had slipped back into the old patterns of sin and Jesus had forgiven her.

"For a righteous man may fall seven times and rise again. But the wicked shall fall by calamity" (Prov. 24:16).

Our problem is that if after being set free from the demons of some specific sin we do not quickly fill the vacuum with good replacements, we will soon fall into the old ruts of behavior.

"When an unclean spirit goes out of a man, he goes through dry places, seeking rest; and finding none, he says, 'I will return to my house from which I came.' And when he comes, he finds it swept and put in order. Then he goes and takes with him seven other spirits more wicked than himself, and they enter and dwell there; and the last state of that man is worse than the first" (Luke 11:24-26).

These seven devils represent the seven areas in which Mary needed to obtain victory. You have heard the expression "the seven deadly sins"? Though that is not very biblical, the Scriptures do hint at seven areas in which God's children must gain the victory.

"These six things the Lord hates, yes, seven are an abomination to Him" (Prov. 6:16). They are as follows:

1. "A proud look" (verse 17).
2. "A lying tongue" (verse 17).

3. "Hands that shed innocent blood" (verse 17).
4. "A heart that devises wicked plans" (verse 18).
5. "Feet that are swift in running to evil" (verse 18).
6. "A false witness who speaks lies" (verse 19).
7. "One who sows discord among brethren" (verse 19).

If, like Mary, you find yourself repenting of the same sin several times, do not despair. Jesus said in Luke 17:3, 4: "Take heed to yourselves. If your brother sins against you, rebuke him; and if he repents, forgive him. And if he sins against you seven times in a day, and seven times in a day returns to you, saying, 'I repent,' you shall forgive him."

If God asks us to forgive each other seven times in one day, will He do any less for us? God will forgive us every time we sincerely repent. However, there is a danger that we can come to the place where we presume upon His grace and abuse His forgiveness, hardening our hearts to His love and quenching the sparks of conviction.

There is effort involved in denying self and living the Christian life. The Bible says we war, wrestle, run, fight, and strive. But the fight is a good fight of faith. We strive to trust God's plan and will for us rather than our own. We fight to stay close to Jesus. Like Mary, we are safe from sin when we stay with Jesus. "Whoever abides in Him does not sin" (1 John 3:6).

Mary met Jesus in the Temple that day, and for the first time in her life she found a Man who loved her unconditionally. She met a Man who was more interested in her soul than her body. From the moment she heard Him say "Neither do I condemn you; go and sin no more" (John 8:11), she understood He would somehow take her place as the condemned. She saw the glaring, murderous looks of the priests and knew that they would not rest until they had revenge for their humiliation before the people. In the Temple that day Christ stood between a guilty, condemned woman and her accusers. He would bear her punishment. This is also what Jesus has done for each one of us.

AT JESUS' FEET IN SORROW:

CHAPTER

"PRAYING FOR THE DEAD"

TWO

The Story

Lazarus' labored breathing was slowing now. Mary's ailing brother had been slipping in and out of consciousness throughout the night. By morning his body quivered with fever; his eyes were open and locked in position.

Where's Jesus? Mary wondered to herself. *What's taking Him so long?* The urgent message was sent four days ago. By now He should be here!

The messenger had found Jesus and returned. "The Master said, 'This sickness is not unto death, but for the glory of God, that the Son of God may be glorified by it'" (John 11:4, NASB).

At first the man's words buoyed Mary's flagging spirits. But as the hours passed and Lazarus' condition worsened, doubts nibbled at the corners of her mind.

"Not unto death, not unto death." Mary repeated the words in her heart like a chant for reassurance, though her eyes and ears told her that her only brother was just moments from death. She watched as her older sister, Martha, bathed Lazarus' fevered forehead and beard with a cool cloth, occasionally leaning closer to her unconscious brother's ear and whispering, "The Master will be here soon, and all will be well. Please hold on."

Mary knew Martha repeated this more for her benefit now, because Lazarus had stopped responding to their comments during the long night.

Several months had passed since Mary had first met Jesus during the shameful episode in the Temple and begun to follow Him. Mary had gone directly from the Temple to Martha and Lazarus' home in Bethany, two miles away. Crying tears of repentance, she confessed the whole strange incident to her family. She openly told them of the secret life of sin she had been living and how Jesus had forgiven her.

Mary wondered out loud, "Could this Rabbi from Nazareth be the Messiah? The One we've waited for for so long?"

News of the Teacher had already touched the hearts of Martha and Lazarus. They were already convinced of the divine mission of Jesus of Nazareth, and they were not surprised by Mary's confession. Her siblings had firm suspicions as to the reasons Mary had moved up to the town of Magdala.

Magdala was an infamous city located on the western shore of the Sea of Galilee. It was a Roman resort town, frequented by soldiers on leave. Brightly lit pleasure boats loaded with reveling soldiers, loose women, and an abundance of wine would launch from the docks in Magdala nightly. Their loud music and drunken laughter were the bane of the local fishermen.

For years Mary had told Martha and Lazarus a partial truth, that she earned her keep by repairing clothing for the military. They'd seen the large sums of money their sister brought on each visit—much more than a sewer would earn.

Daily Martha and Lazarus prayed for their sister's deliverance from her immoral life. They believed that just as Jehovah had transformed Rahab the harlot into a respected mother in Israel, He could save Mary. Their gratitude overflowed for this sudden change in their younger sister. Mary's eyes were bright and happy for the first time in years.

That same afternoon Lazarus sought out and found Jesus, then insisted that He and His friends come home for dinner. Jesus agreed, and by the end of the evening Martha and her brother persuaded Jesus and His friends to stay in their home whenever they found themselves in the area.

Many people eagerly came to hear Jesus teach, but few invited Him into their home. The Pharisees and Sadducees had persuaded the Jewish people to consider Jesus a dangerous enemy of their faith.

To invite Him to their home would be certain social suicide and incur the wrath of the local synagogue leaders.

Jesus warned Lazarus about the potential pitfalls of hosting One so hated, but Lazarus was undaunted. He repeated that his spacious home was open to Jesus and His disciples anytime. The Teacher gratefully accepted the man's act of hospitality.

Soon it became evident that the Master felt drawn to this trio of siblings. The home of Lazarus and Martha became a regular oasis from the busy pressures of His ministry. Jesus cherished the clean, orderly environment that surrounded Martha.

As fellow carpenters, Lazarus and Jesus would exchange wood-working techniques. Also, the Master found Mary's simple hunger for truth refreshing compared to the constant resistance from the scribes and religious leaders.

Thus began a strong friendship between Jesus, Lazarus, Martha, and Mary. They became His family whenever He was in the vicinity of Jerusalem. This would be the only place during Jesus' earthly ministry where He could enjoy the conveniences of a relaxed home and the warmth of a family. He and His disciples often took refuge in the Bethany home, except when the weather was mild. Then Jesus preferred sleeping under the stars in a secluded olive orchard just outside of Jerusalem—a place called Gethsemane.

Considering Jesus' great love for her brother, Mary found it hard to imagine that the Master would not rush to His friend's side when He heard of Lazarus' illness. Suddenly the uneven rhythm of Lazarus' breathing stopped. Martha and Mary fastened their gaze on the still form of their beloved brother. In the deafening silence, their minds shouted, *Breathe! Breathe!*

Almost as if he could hear the unspoken plea of their hearts, Lazarus took one more short breath, then slowly released it. For a moment silence hung in the sickroom like a heavy dark garment. Suddenly the long unbearable silence was broken by the chilling wail of grief that came first from deep within Martha, then from Mary. There by his cot, the bed linens damp from his fever, the two women fell to their knees and sobbed and cried as their brother's warm body cooled.

Where was Jesus? He had healed so many strangers with no effort. Why had He not come to heal His friend? All the times Lazarus and Martha welcomed Him into their home, fed and sheltered His motley tribe of disciples, and He had not come when He was needed. Questions and doubts nibbled away at the minds of the two sisters.

After a time Martha stood up and resolutely wiped her eyes with a cloth. "We must make arrangements," she said, jutting her chin forward in determination. Martha found relief in activity. In their confidence that Jesus would come and heal Lazarus, they had never expected him to die, and hence had made no preparations.

"I need to go to the market to buy the burial cloth and the necessary ointments," Martha said as she dabbed her eyes with a cloth. Since Mary's embarrassing ordeal in the Temple, the younger sister seldom ventured into town.

Moving toward the door, Martha turned toward Mary. "We have no grave," she said. As the word "grave" came from her lips, her voice broke and fresh tears began to flow.

Mary wrapped her arms around her older sister. "What about the land outside of Bethany that our parents left us? Lazarus loved sitting on the rock atop the hill."

"I know, but the ground there is almost solid rock. It would take several men a week or more to dig even a shallow grave," Martha reminded.

"True. But as I remember, there are caves in the side of the hill. I used to play in them as a girl," Mary admitted. "For that matter, I know of one cave that would be big enough to bury a king."

Martha's brow knitted. She pursed her lips as she thought about her sister's suggestion. "A cave would be better than a hole in the ground. Father Abraham was buried in a cave, and Lazarus has been noble as any king. A good suggestion. We'll use the cave."

With the place of interment decided, Martha switched into action. "Mary, I need you to go to Jabin's family and tell them of our loss. They're the best mourners in the valley. Ask them to come to our home early tomorrow morning, with a few other mourners. And we will hire some musicians as well." She buzzed from the room, talking as she walked. "I'll arrange for the ruler of the synagogue to say the prayers before you and I lead the procession to the grave."

That the funeral went well was no surprise. Whenever Martha took charge of an event, the occasion always went well. The woman was known throughout the region as a consummate organizer, an expert at handling details.

On the second day several of their cousins arrived from the north and joined the hired mourners. Martha and Mary appreciated the comfort they received from family and friends. But every now and then someone would say, "I thought you were good friends with the Rabbi healer from Galilee. I would have expected to see Him here. It's too bad He didn't come in time to heal dear Lazarus."

With each such remark, painful confusion made a fresh twist in their hearts. Why hadn't He come? Why had God allowed their brother to die? Martha questioned the messenger again and again. "Are you sure He understood you?"

"Yes, yes," the young man said. "The Rabbi told me that Lazarus' sickness was not unto death, but for the glory of God, that the Son of God may be glorified through it. That's just what He said."

So why, then, did He not come? Had He met with tragedy on His way to Bethany? Had the Jews arrested Him? Was the Master languishing in a filthy Roman jail cell, as had His older cousin, John the Baptist?

On the morning of the fourth day Martha had just finished feeding her household of visiting family members and guests when one of her cousins burst into the kitchen. The boy whispered something to Martha: "One of Jesus' disciples asked me to tell you that Jesus is waiting for you outside the village."

Knowing the Lord had many enemies near Jerusalem, and wanting to avoid attracting undue attention, Martha quietly slipped away from the house without telling Mary. She followed the young boy to an olive grove outside Bethany.

Martha saw Jesus sitting on the stone edge of an olive press, resting from His journey. Running to Him, she knelt before Him and with broken sobs said, "Lord, if You had been here, my brother would not have died" (John 11:21).

This was as much a question as a statement. She gazed into Jesus' face and read something completely unanticipated. Where she'd expected to find sorrow she found peace and joy. A flicker of hope suddenly flamed in Martha's mind. Jesus had raised the dead before. There was that young girl near Capernaum. Of course, the scribes had said that she was not really dead. Just in a deep sleep. But Peter, James, and John, who witnessed the child's resurrection, assured her that the girl had been completely cold, still, and lifeless. And when Jesus had said "Little girl, I say to you, get up!" the child had come back to life.

Then Martha recalled hearing about the son of that poor widow from Nain. The young man was already being carried off for burial when Jesus stopped the procession and touched the coffin, forcing the bearers to come to a halt. Then He said, "Young man, I say to you, arise!" (Luke 7:14). And there in the middle of the street, the dead boy sat up and spoke to his mother.

Could Jesus do this for Lazarus even after four days? Martha summoned every ounce of faith before speaking. "Even now, I know that whatever You ask of God, God will give You" (John 11:22).

Jesus placed His hand tenderly on her shoulder and gazed lovingly into the grieving woman's tear-stained face. "Your brother will rise again," He said (verse 23).

Wanting to be certain that she and Jesus were speaking of the same event, Martha replied, "I know that he will rise again in the resurrection at the last day" (verse 24).

Now it was Jesus' turn to clarify the issue. For if He did resurrect Lazarus, it would be only a temporary extension of this earthly life. Then he would die again. But the life Jesus had come to give was one that has no end.

Jesus said to her, "I am the resurrection and the life; he who believes in Me shall live even if he dies, and everyone who lives and believes in Me shall never die. Do you believe this?" (verses 25, 26, NASB). His question cut her to the quick. She recalled the doubts she had been entertaining since Lazarus died. Faith was always the supreme issue with the Master.

With conviction Martha said, "Yes, Lord; I have believed that

You are the Christ, the Son of God, even He who comes into the world" (verse 27, NASB).

Jesus tenderly took Martha's hands in His. "Go quietly and bring Mary with you. We will go to the tomb together."

Martha immediately made her way back to the house, moving as fast as she could without giving the appearance of running. As she skipped over stones in her pathway, reservations arose in her mind. *Yes, Jesus raised the dead, but those people had been dead for only a few hours. Lazarus has been dead four days now.*

She shook loose the unwelcome doubt from her thinking. *I must believe He can do even this.* As she approached the house things were quiet, aside from the hushed weeping of the mourners. The weary musicians were taking a break from their cycle of prayers and woeful tunes.

Martha spotted Mary sitting on the edge of a bench by the window, rocking her upper body back and forth, and gazing at nothing in particular. She had drawn a black shawl over her hair and shoulders. She seemed to be embracing herself as if she were cold, even though there was a warm afternoon breeze. The younger woman's lips moved, but no words came out. Martha placed her hand gently on Mary's back and whispered in her ear. "The Teacher is here. He's calling for you."

Martha hoped not to arouse the attention of the scribes at the funeral. Everyone knew they were siding with the priests against the Galilean Healer.

But when Mary heard her sister's message, she inhaled sharply. The younger sister sprang to her feet and rushed out of the house. She had just been praying that Jesus would come.

The Jews who were in the house consoling her watched Mary flee. And Martha ran after her. Assuming the two sisters were going to the tomb to weep, they followed, saying to one another, "This is the last day of mourning. We should join them."

Jesus was still sitting patiently in the place where Martha had met Him. When Mary saw Him she collapsed at His feet and sobbed, "Lord, if You had been here, my brother would not have died" (verse 32).

When Jesus saw her tears and those of the hired mourners who were slowly climbing the trail, He felt their pain. Tenderly He brushed away a teardrop from the woman's cheek. He bowed His head and closed His eyes. It was as though a supernatural agony weighed down upon Him. A heart-wrenching groan escaped His lips. Then He lifted her face to meet His own and asked, "Where have you laid him?" (verse 34).

Martha responded, "Lord, come and see" (verse 34).

As Jesus and the women entered the clearing at the foot of the hill, the mourners and musicians soon stationed themselves behind the family, facing the grave. The hired mourners launched into a fresh demonstration of first-class grieving, and the musicians accompanied with doleful funeral dirges. They wanted to impress the famous Rabbi with their depth of emotion.

Tears welled up in the Teacher's eyes; those involuntary muscles of grief contorted His facial expression. And Jesus wept.

One of the scribes, startled by this authentic demonstration of grief, sarcastically blurted out, "Could not He who opened the eyes of the blind have kept this man from dying?"

Jesus heard the man's remark and looked up, His face wet with tears. After the Master regained His poise He gazed at the large stone covering the cave. There the cold remains of His friend lay decomposing in darkness. He knew that before long, His own lifeless body would be sealed in a similar fashion.

Just as the mourners' wailing cries and shrill music reached a new crescendo, Jesus stunned the gathering. "Take away the stone," He called out loudly (verse 39). Instantly the weeping and wailing stopped and was followed by a long awkward silence. The entire assembly stood speechless, looking at Jesus, then at Martha. Not wanting to be tasteless about such things in front of her guests, Martha wanted to be sure she understood her Lord's request. As gracefully as possible, she cast Him a worried smile. "Master," she said, "by this time there is a bad odor. He has been there four days."

A slight smile teased the corners of the Master's lips. "Did I not tell you that if you believed, you would see the glory of God?"

Martha's breath caught in her throat as she slowly turned toward Mary for approval. Mary nodded eagerly. Taking a deep breath for courage, Martha motioned to some of the robust young men who had helped prepare the cave a few days earlier. "Do as He says."

They found the lever poles that had been used to roll the massive stone over the entrance of the tomb. Glancing one final time at the sisters, the men hoped the women would reconsider this morbid request. Instead they saw a settled determination in the women's expressions.

While two men pulled down on the long pole wedged at the base of the stone, another pushed with his back against the rock. The men pushed until the boulder rolled three feet to the left, exposing the entrance of Lazarus' grave.

The men might have moved the stone farther, but the overwhelming stench of death wafting out of the cave entrance sent them gagging from the hillside sepulcher.

With royal dignity Jesus raised His head and stretched His hands toward the heavens. "Father, I thank You that You have heard Me. And I know that You always hear Me, but because of the people who are standing by I said this, that they may believe that You sent Me" (verses 41, 42). Then with authority and confidence, He fastened His gaze on the tomb and called in loud trumpet-clear tones, "Lazarus, come out!"

For a few moments time stood still. Every eye was riveted on the tomb. From the darkness of the cave came a muffled sound and the shadow of some movement. Yelps and terrified gasps rippled through the crowd as everyone took a step back—everyone except Mary and Martha, who had begun approaching the tomb.

From inside the tomb the distinct sound of rustling and a confused muffled voice could be heard, followed by an eerie image that filled the entrance. A man wrapped in yellow graveclothes struggled with bound hands to free his face, at the same time stumbling over the strands of cloth that unraveled from about his feet.

Shrieks arose throughout the crowd of people. Jesus called to some of the terrified spectators, "Loose him, and let him go" (verse 44). Martha was the first to reach Lazarus. Joyfully she tore away the fabric she'd tenderly wrapped around his dead body four days earlier. Mary also rushed to her brother. But before reaching him, she deliberately turned to Jesus and again fell at His feet and poured out her thanks through tears of happiness.

Behind the reunited family the crowd whispered, "This Man must be the Christ!" Unnoticed by the astonished assembly, two of the guests quietly backed away from the funeral-turned-celebration.

"The priests must immediately hear about this fantastic miracle."

The Study

JOHN 11:1-4

"Now a certain man was sick, Lazarus of Bethany, the town of Mary and her sister Martha. It was that Mary who anointed the Lord with fragrant oil and wiped His feet with her hair, whose brother Lazarus was sick. Therefore the sisters sent to Him, saying, 'Lord, behold, he whom You love is sick.' When Jesus heard that, He said, 'This sickness is not unto death, but for the glory of God, that the Son of God may be glorified through it' " (John 11:1-4). (Please read the entire chapter.)

A PATTERN OF GREATNESS

It is interesting to note that the seven resurrections associated with Jesus seem to have happened in a particular order and with increasing drama and power.

First, there was the little girl who had been dead only a few hours (Mark 5:35-43).

Then there was the young man who was being carried off for burial (Luke 7:12-16).

Next was the miracle of Lazarus' resurrection; he had been dead four days (John 11).

Then the miracle of Jesus' rising, which was accompanied by the resurrection of many saints around Jerusalem; they had been dead for years (Matthew 27:51-53).

Next will be the dead in Christ, who rise when He comes in glory (1 Thess. 4:16).

The final resurrection will include the largest number ever. The lost of all ages will be raised for judgment and punishment at the conclusion of the 1,000 years (Rev. 20:5).

PRAYING FOR THE DEAD IN SIN

The raising of Lazarus was doubtless among the most dramatic and striking miracles of Jesus' earthly ministry. The story may have been omitted by the other Gospel writers because they wrote their histories while Lazarus was still alive; perhaps they did not mention him for fear of further exciting the malice of the Jewish leaders. John 12:10, 11 states that Jesus' enemies sought to put Lazarus to death, to remove the living monument of Christ's power and goodness that remained in the land.

But there is much more to learn from this story than the fact that Jesus has power to give new life to inanimate matter. Martin Luther said, "God creates out of nothing. Therefore, until a man is nothing, God can make nothing out of him." Before Jesus can give us new spiritual life we must first die to self, or be "crucified with Christ" (Gal. 2:20).

In the Bible the term *death* is often a symbol for the absence of spiritual life. God told Adam and Eve, "Of the tree of the knowledge of good and evil you shall not eat, for in the day that you eat of it you shall surely die" (Gen. 2:17). Not only did Adam and Eve begin to die physically the day they ate the forbidden fruit; more important, they died spiritually. From that day to this, all of Adam's children are born spiritually dead; they must be born a second time in Jesus.

"Wherefore, as by one man [Adam] sin entered into the world, and death by sin; and so death passed upon all men" (Rom. 5:12).

"Jesus said to him, 'Let the dead bury their own dead, but you go and preach the kingdom of God'" (Luke 9:60).

Until we are born again we are controlled by the lower nature, thus are spiritually dead. "And you He made alive, who were dead in trespasses and sins" (Eph. 2:1). "We know that we have passed from death to life, because we love the brethren. He who does not love his brother abides in death" (1 John 3:14).

Every lost person sits on "death row," as it were, simply waiting for judgment. "He that hath the Son hath life; and he that hath not the Son of God hath not life" (1 John 5:12, KJV).

With these scriptures in mind, remember that Mary is a type or symbol of the church; just as she knelt at Jesus' feet weeping for her brother, the church must spend time praying and, yes, even weeping at the feet of Jesus, asking Him to resurrect our brothers and sisters who are spiritually dead. When we do this we can expect the same results that Mary and Martha received—new spiritual life for our loved ones. Jesus said, "I am the resurrection and the life. He who believes in Me, though he may die, he shall live" (John 11:25). This is the good news.

This means more than the physical resurrection upon Jesus' return. Only those who in this life experience a spiritual death, burial, and resurrection will be prepared for the physical resurrection at Jesus' coming.

Those born only once will die twice. This of course means the second death, referred to in Revelation 20:14. But he who is born twice will die only once—he that is born physically and then spiritually will experience the physical death only once.

PERSEVERING PRAYER

Just as Mary pleaded and cried at Jesus' feet for the resurrection of her brother, the New Testament church was also resurrected through the prayers and tears of Paul and others like him. "I thank God, whom I serve with a pure conscience, as my forefathers did, as without ceasing I remember you in my prayers night and day" (2 Tim. 1:3). "For out of much affliction and anguish of heart I wrote to you, with many tears, not that you should be grieved, but that you might know the love which I have so abundantly for you" (2 Cor. 2:4).

We must also pray and plead persistently that God will grant life to our lost friends and loved ones. Elijah prayed three times before the dead child rose, and seven times for the rain to come (1 Kings 17:21; 18:43). James 5:16 says, "The effective, fervent prayer of a righteous man avails much." "For in due season we shall reap if we do not lose heart" (Gal. 6:9).

Admiral Robert E. Peary was victorious in his quest for the North Pole only because he was persistent. He searched for many years. The Inuits told him, "You are like the sun. You always come back." His dominating desire led him to persevere in spite of physical, financial, and natural difficulties. Later he said, "For 24 years, sleeping or awake, to place the stars and stripes on the Pole has been my dream."

Should we be less persistent when praying for eternal victories? Through perseverance the snail reached the ark, and small drops of water wear out a large stone.

I know one woman who prayed for 50 years for the conversion of her spouse; then he was dramatically converted!

Like Mary, our persistent prayers that Jesus will spiritually resurrect our lost friends and family will be rewarded.

WHEN IS THE RESURRECTION?

We can't rush past this subject of Lazarus' death and resurrection without considering some popular yet very dangerous misconceptions regarding the state of human beings in death.

Many have been falsely taught that as soon as a person dies he or she is instantly ushered into his or her reward, directly to heaven or hell. This teaching had its origins in ancient pagan religions; it is not based on Scripture.

Remember when Martha said, "I know that he will rise again in the resurrection at the last day" (John 11:24)? The general resurrection of the dead in Christ on the great judgment day and the giving of just rewards do not take place until the second coming of Jesus. Here are a few scriptures to consider:

"This is the will of the Father who sent Me, that of all He has given Me I should lose nothing, but should raise it up at the last day" (John 6:39).

"No one can come to Me unless the Father who sent Me draws him; and I will raise him up at the last day" (verse 44).

If a person is catapulted right into heaven or hell at the time of death, then what is the need for the judgment and resurrection at the end of the world?

Jesus will awaken the dead upon His return. In 1 Thessalonians 4:16-18 Paul tells us, "The Lord Himself will descend from heaven with a shout, with the voice of an archangel, and with the trumpet of God. And the dead in Christ will rise first. Then we who are alive and remain shall be caught up together with them in the clouds to meet the Lord in the air. And thus we shall always be with the Lord. Therefore comfort one another with these words."

Again, Paul refers to this resurrection in 1 Corinthians 15:23: "But each one in his own order: Christ the firstfruits, afterward those who are Christ's [will rise] *at His coming.*" And in Revelation 22:12

John writes, "And behold, I am coming quickly, and My reward is with Me, to give to every one according to his work." You can see that Jesus distributes the rewards when He comes!

NO COMMENT!

Remember, Lazarus did not report, after being dead for four days then resurrected, that Jesus snatched him back from the portals of glory and from a heavenly communion of angels to return to this dark world. That would be a dirty trick, don't you think? Neither did Lazarus thank Jesus for saving him from the blistering fires of hell or from the discomfort of purgatory.

If this resurrection were to happen in our day, the first thing all the news reporters would ask Lazarus as they shoved a hundred microphones in his face would be "What did you see after death?" "What did you experience?"

Incredibly, Lazarus made no comment at all on his after-death experience. Why? Because he had none! The Bible teaches that death is a form of dreamless sleep, a rest after pain. This is why Jesus said, "Our friend Lazarus sleeps, but I go that I may wake him up" (John 11:11).

When Jesus raised the little girl He said, "The child is not dead, but sleeping" (Mark 5:39).

Consider these other scriptures that illustrate that in death a person is not thinking or conscious: "The living know that they shall die: but the dead know not any thing" (Eccl. 9:5, KJV). "Whatever your hand finds to do, do it with your might; for there is no work or device or knowledge or wisdom in the grave where you are going" (verse 10). "The dead praise not the Lord, neither any that go down into silence" (Ps. 115:17, KJV). "Put not your trust in princes, nor in the son of man, in whom there is no help. His breath goeth forth, he returneth to his earth; in that very day his thoughts perish" (Ps. 146:3, 4, KJV).

The Bible is exceedingly clear regarding man's unconscious state in death. Yet many believe that if you hit a Christian in the head with a hammer and knock him unconscious, he knows nothing; but if you hit him a little harder so that he dies, he is ushered into heaven and knows everything! Does that make sense?

ABSENT FROM THE BODY?

But Doug, you may ask, what about that scripture that says "we are confident, yes, well pleased rather to be absent from the body and to be present with the Lord" (2 Cor. 5:8)? Doesn't this passage mean that as soon as a saved person dies he or she is ushered into God's presence? My answer is yes and no. I know that sounds like I am running for public office, but stay with me.

Keep in mind that there is no awareness of time in death; when a saint dies his or her next conscious thought will be of the resurrection and God's presence. A thousand years may have passed on Planet Earth, but the dead don't know about it! For them it seems as "in a moment, in the twinkling of an eye, at the last trumpet. For the trumpet will sound, and the dead will be raised incorruptible, and we shall be changed" (1 Cor. 15:52).

On the day of Pentecost, Peter said, regarding good king David: "Men and brethren, let me speak freely to you of the patriarch David, that he is both dead and buried, and his tomb is with us to this day. . . . For David did not ascend into the heavens" (Acts 2:29-34).

Forty days after Jesus' resurrection, Peter said that David, who had been dead 1,000 years, was still asleep in his grave and had not yet ascended to heaven. Three thousand years have now passed since David's death, but that godly man has no awareness of this time. When Jesus returns, it will seem but a moment to the mighty king. After closing his eyes in death, the next thing David will be aware of is the resurrection, his new glorified body, and being in God's presence.

THE RICH MAN AND LAZARUS

Another scripture that is often cited in an attempt to prove that the dead go right to heaven or hell after death and before the resurrection or judgment is the parable of the rich man and Lazarus, found in Luke 16:19-31. The main question before us on this matter is whether this story about the rich man and Lazarus is literally true or a parable. Here are four reasons that it could not possibly be literalistic:

1. The beggar died and was taken by the angels to Abraham's bosom. No one believes that Abraham's literal bosom is the abode of

the righteous dead. It would hardly be big enough. This is a figurative or parabolic expression. Incidentally, the angels *will* gather the saints, but according to Matthew 24:31 this will take place at the coming of Jesus, not at a person's death.

2. Heaven and hell are depicted in this parable as separated by a gulf, and yet the persons in each could converse with each other. There are probably few individuals in the world who believe that this will be literally true of the saved and the lost (Luke 16:26).

3. The rich man was in hell with a physical body. He had eyes, a tongue, etc. (verses 23, 24). How did his body get into hellfire instead of into the grave? I know of no one who teaches that the bodies of the wicked go into hell as soon as they die. This story could not be literal.

4. The request for Lazarus to dip the tip of his finger in water and come through the flames to cool the rich man's tongue is obviously not literal. How much moisture would be left and how much relief would it give?

The whole story is unrealistic and parabolic. The rich man in the parable undoubtedly represented the Jewish nation, because only a Jew would pray to "Father Abraham." The beggar symbolized the Gentiles, who were counted unworthy to receive the truth. The very name Lazarus (Laz' uh ruhs) means "one whom God helps" *(Holman Bible Dictionary)*. In Matthew 15:27 the Canaanite mother acknowledged that her people, the Gentiles, were beggars at the table of the Jews. The Jewish nation feasted on the word of God while Gentiles around them starved for a few crumbs of truth, much like many professed Christian churches today.

Possibly Christ chose to use the name of Lazarus in the parable because He knew He would later actually raise Lazarus from the dead. The climactic point of the entire parable, the main meaning Christ intended, is found in Luke 16:31: "If they hear not Moses and the prophets, neither will they be persuaded, though one rose from the dead" (KJV). Sure enough, they didn't believe even when one named Lazarus was raised before them.

A COMMA THIEF

Perhaps someone else is thinking, *Didn't Jesus promise the thief on the cross, "Today you will be with Me in Paradise"* (Luke 23:43)?

Sorry, that's not what He said. As the Greek was originally written, there was no punctuation. That refinement on literature did not develop for centuries after the writing of the Bible. Later translators had to decide where to put periods and commas. Since the popular teaching was that a person went directly to heaven or hell upon death, there was a strong political reason for translators to place the comma before the word "today" instead of after, completely changing the meaning of the verse.

A misplaced comma can communicate a totally opposite meaning than what is intended. For example, in the 1920s a wealthy stock trader sent his wife to Paris with some friends for her birthday. Before her return, she sent a Western Union telegram to her husband asking permission to purchase a stunning fox coat that cost $1,000. Her husband wired back his response: "No price too high." Thrilled by her husband's benevolence, she purchased the beautiful white coat.

When her husband met her at the ship, she disembarked wearing her lavish new acquisition. Her outraged spouse inquired, "Why did you buy the coat? I told you it was too expensive!"

Bewildered, she replied, "But honey, you said no price was too high."

He shook his head. "I said no, the price is too high!"

The telegraph office had neglected to put the comma after the word "no."

We know that the thief could not have ascended to Paradise with Jesus the day of the Crucifixion, because in John 20:17 Jesus said to Mary, "Do not cling to Me, for I have not yet ascended to My Father; but go to My brethren and say to them, 'I am ascending to My Father and your Father, and to My God and your God.'" This statement was made on Sunday morning beside the tomb. Jesus spoke to the thief on Friday afternoon. How could the thief be with Jesus in Paradise on Friday if the crucified Lord still had not ascended to the Father by Sunday morning?

If we place the comma after the word "today," everything falls into place. Jesus was emphasizing that "while I do not look like a

Lord or a king, I am promising you today, that you will be with Me in Paradise."

NOW IS THE TIME TO PRAY

In numerous religions of the world, people engage in burning candles and praying for the souls of their dead loved ones and ancestors. The Bible is clear that once a person dies his or her case is closed. He or she goes to the grave with his or her sins either covered by the blood of Jesus or exposed, and waits for reward or punishment.

"It is appointed unto men once to die, but after this the judgment" (Heb. 9:27, KJV). "And the dead were judged according to their works, by the things which were written in the books" (Rev. 20:12).

No amount of prayers or intercession from the living will alter a person's case once he or she is dead. However, the good news is that we can make a difference now by praying and weeping at Jesus' feet for those who are dead in sin.

FREE FROM THE DIRTY, DEAD RAGS

One final point to ponder in the story of Lazarus' resurrection is that after Jesus raised Lazarus He commanded that Lazarus be loosed from the old death rags that bound him. Isa. 64:6 says, "But we are all like an unclean thing, and all our righteousnesses are like filthy rags." Jesus came to give us life and freedom from the bondage of eternal death. "And he that was dead came forth, bound hand and foot with graveclothes: and his face was bound about with a napkin. Jesus saith unto them, Loose him, and let him go" (John 11:44, KJV).

Jesus came to give us life instead of death. He sets us free from the filthy, unrighteous death rags that imprison us, and He covers us with the pure robe of His own righteousness.

"MARTHA'S DISTRACTIONS"

The Story

Spellbound, Mary sat at Jesus' feet in Martha's home, listening as the Lord shared the good news about the principles of His kingdom and the limitless love of His heavenly Father. She would have been more comfortable on a bench across the room, but that was too far from Jesus. Mary wanted to see into His gentle eyes. When He taught, they seemed to reflect an eternity of knowledge. They were so deep and expressive, even divine. Sometimes Mary was embarrassed when she realized she was staring at His eyes. Mary thought she could just fall into Jesus' eyes and drown in the love she saw there.

Usually Jesus was surrounded by His disciples and the teeming multitudes. Whenever He visited her home in Bethany, only the disciples remained. She cherished the rare moments when she could be close to Him without the demands and distractions of the multitude. She had so many questions to ask. Yet she knew it would not be appropriate for a woman, especially a woman with her reputation, to ask Jesus any questions in public. Here in her sister's parlor, Mary thought she would be free from censure.

After Jesus raised her brother from the dead, Mary moved down from Magdala to live with Martha and Lazarus in Bethany. For a time she had tried to maintain her place in that northern Roman resort town because Jesus spent much more time teaching up by the Sea of Galilee than in Jerusalem. But Mary had learned the hard way how weak she was when separated from the Master. Back in her old environment of Magdala, associating with friends and acquaintances from the past life, she quickly succumbed to old temptations. Several nights, after being enticed back into sin, Mary would sit alone in the dim glow of the oil lamp and cry, scooping her tears from her cheeks with her tear jar.

Like others in her era, Mary had purchased a blue glass flask with a funnel-like lip on top with which to catch her tears of shame and sorrow. Mary's fountain of pain was so deep that two times she had had to buy a bigger flask to contain her tears.

This was her liquid diary. Seven times, while living in Magdala, Mary sought out Jesus and asked Him to forgive her and to rescue her from the demons of guilt and lust that bound her. And Jesus always did. The seventh time she knelt at Jesus' feet in shame, He told the listening crowd a parable. Mary knew the story was meant especially for her.

"When an unclean spirit goes out of a man, he goes through dry places, seeking rest; and finding none, he says, 'I will return to my house from which I came.' And when he comes, he finds it swept and put in order. Then he goes and takes with him seven other spirits more wicked than himself, and they enter and dwell there; and the last state of that man is worse than the first" (Luke 11:24-26).

Jesus was telling Mary that she needed a new beginning. She needed to fill her life with new friends and a new environment, or the old devils would continue to return. So she sold her house in Magdala, and all the jewels and gifts the soldiers had given her. She took her expensive risqué garments used to attract customers and burned them at the city dump.

With only her flask of tears, a few modest clothes in a bag, and a substantial purse of money, she made the 75-mile trip to Martha and Lazarus' home in Bethany. When Mary turned her back on the old life she felt a great peace. This victory would be permanent. As Jesus had often said, she "put her hand to the plow and did not look back."

Sitting at Jesus' feet, Mary listened eagerly as He taught her. The Teacher smiled at her, encouraging her to ask her simple but profound questions.

A fresh cloud of dust wafted from the bottom of Martha's dress every time she rushed past her guests. Martha had a way of running with her shoulders back and head up so she did not appear to be running. Dashing through the house would not look dignified and, if nothing else, Martha was very conscious of appearances, especially when Jesus was visiting.

From the scruffiest scamp on the street to the most dignified lawyer, all of Bethany knew that later that day Jesus would be dining at Simon's house. Anybody who was anybody in the village would be there, not only because Jesus would be there, but because Lazarus, the man raised from the dead, would be there.

A short time earlier they'd witnessed his cold, still body, wrapped in aloe-soaked graveclothes, committed to the dark tomb on the hillside outside Bethany. Then Jesus had come and astonished the whole region by miraculously raising him to life. But perhaps the main reason people clamored to attend the feast was Uncle Simon himself.

For years Uncle Simon, a Pharisee, had been one of the most prosperous and respected citizens of Bethany. Then one morning the gossip spread through the town that the Temple priests had pronounced that their uncle had contracted leprosy—a virtual sentence of death.

Leprosy was a most devastating and dreaded scourge, sometimes known as the "curse," or "finger of God." When Martha told Mary about Uncle Simon's condition, she added, "There must have been some sin in his life. Otherwise God would not do this to Uncle Simon." Martha shook her head and clicked her tongue. "Women!" Rumor was that Simon had a problem with young women.

Mary dropped her eyes and said nothing. She knew all too well about Uncle Simon's problem. He had been the one to lead his pretty niece down the spiraling road of disgrace. Mary kept this shameful secret buried deep in her past.

Uncle Simon was a typical Pharisee of his era. He preached by the mile and lived by the inch. He talked like a priest in public and lived like a publican, a tax collector, in the shadows.

After the priests pronounced Simon a leper, he was driven from the village to live with the other lepers in the "camp of the dead." These colonies were the most wretched, pitiful, and de-spairing places on earth. Buzzards circled above the compounds, watching and waiting for leprosy's victims. The colonies were places where men, women, and children, torn away from their families by this cursed disease, were sent to die by slow degree, suffering from infected sores, missing limbs, and blindness before their ultimate demise.

Simon had been afflicted with a hopeless case of leprosy for so long that he'd been nicknamed Simon the leper. Faithfully Martha brought Simon food. She would set the basket down outside the camp and call to him. Martha knew she must keep a stone's throw away from her uncle. As to the basket, it could never be used again by "clean" people.

Martha did not mind the sacrifice of her time and effort. She en-joyed serving people. On each visit she tried to persuade Uncle Simon to go to Jesus, but he refused, certain God had forsaken him.

On one such visit Martha shouted a message that brought a glim-mer of hope to Simon. "Uncle Simon, I heard that the Teacher healed a man from leprosy in Galilee."

A desperate desire glimmered in Simon's heart. Martha added, "If the Teacher could raise Lazarus after four days in the grave, He could certainly heal you! Go to Him," Martha urged. "He won't turn you away."

When Simon returned to the colony he told his fellow sufferers what Martha had said. "If the Man has healed and forgiven other lepers, then perhaps He can heal me, too. I'm going to find this Jesus and beg for cleansing. It's worth a try."

Some mocked his absurd plan, but there were nine, including a Samaritan, who insisted on going with him. And so a pitiful parade of lepers began the long journey north to where they had heard Jesus was teaching. With each step they hoped against hope that He would have mercy on them.

At one point the 10 men nearly gave up in despair; they were pelted with stones by a gang of youths, cursing and shouting, "Lepers! Dirty lepers! Cursed of God." Unwittingly the band of lep ers had ventured too close to one of the towns along the way.

When the lepers finally found Jesus and His disciples, He was making His way into a small fishing village. Forbidden to approach the Teacher and His entourage, Simon called out to Him from the brow of a nearby hill, "Jesus! Master, have mercy on us!"

The others, who had cowered behind their leader, joined in the pleading chorus, "Jesus! Master, have mercy on us!"

Once again, demonstrating His amazing love and patience, Jesus told them, "Go, show yourselves to the priests."

At first they were perplexed by this order. They had already been inspected by the priest and declared lepers. But in faith Simon turned to carry out the Master's command. The other nine did the same. As they turned they felt a surge of vitality and strength flash through their bodies. And in an instant the blind eyes were healed, sores disappeared, even missing toes and fingers popped into place. Every trace of leprosy vanished from them all!

They'd been set free! Leaping and praising God, they rushed toward the Temple to find the priests who could declare them healed. In his excitement Simon glanced at the other men as they ran and realized that the Samaritan was no longer with them. Simon figured that since the priest wouldn't pronounce a Samaritan clean, the man had chosen to go home to Samaria. It wasn't until later Simon discovered that the Samaritan was the only one of their group who had returned to thank Jesus for his healing. Jesus commended the Samaritan for doing so.

Convicted of his own ingratitude, Uncle Simon wanted to do something grandiose to demonstrate his appreciation to Jesus. When he heard that Jesus had come to Jerusalem for the Passover, Simon decided to honor Jesus with a lavish feast. He would invite His disciples, too, and of course, the leaders in the community. And who would be better to cater Simon's feast than his niece Martha?

In the Bethany kitchen Martha continued her culinary preparations in a frantic yet organized way. Like everyone else, Mary marveled how her older sister was able to accomplish so much.

A weaver by trade, Martha produced the best and brightest wool carpets in Jerusalem. Mary enjoyed watching Martha's hands fly across the loom with meticulous tight perfection on every warp and woof. In fact, shortly after befriending Jesus, Mary had helped her sister weave a fine, sturdy, seamless robe for Jesus. She had never seen a more beautiful combination of colors in any fabric. Mary surmised that it must have been a robe like this that the patriarch Jacob had given to his son Joseph.

From the time she rose each morning to the moment she dropped off to sleep each night, Martha was a dynamo of activity. Mary would smile as she noted how Martha's kinetic energy made her squirm and fidget in the synagogue each Sabbath as she tried to sit still and listen to the rabbi read from the Scriptures.

However, Martha's gift for leadership and her boundless energy had also been what had intimidated and frightened off male suitors over the years. While Martha would never admit it, Mary sadly knew her sister was wrestling with the secret fear of dying an old maid, of never knowing a man or nursing a baby at her breast.

Martha whisked by Mary and Jesus again, except this time she forced a smile toward Jesus and glared at her younger sister. Mary understood the unspoken message: *Get up and help me. Can't you see how busy I am?*

Please, not now! Mary directed her silent plea, communicating with facial expressions, that only siblings can interpret. The disciples had gone out, and Jesus' conversation with Mary had grown more intense. She sensed He was preparing to share something of vital importance with her.

Of course, Jesus knew they would soon be interrupted again, and Mary must hear His message. The Teacher leaned forward, His eyes saddened. "Mary, the Son of Man is going to be betrayed into the hands of men, and they will kill Him. After He is killed, He will rise the third day."

More than once before, Mary had overheard Jesus make this statement to His disciples, but those 12 men who had followed Him for more than three years never seemed alarmed. It was as if they thought Jesus was speaking in a parable again. But Mary now understood what they did not—Jesus was deliberately being as plain and literal as possible.

She knew He had a growing number of enemies that would not

rest until He was dead. She remembered hearing John the Baptist refer to Jesus as the "Lamb of God that takes away the sin of the world." Didn't His friends know? Didn't they understand that the designated lamb in the Temple rituals, the one that takes away the sins of the people, always dies?

As Mary sat at Jesus' feet the devastating truth of His statement pierced her heart like a Roman spear. Soon Jesus would die for her sins and for the sins of the world. Tears welled up in Mary's eyes and trickled down her face. As He studied her eyes, He searched her soul. Just as she knew He would be dying for her, Jesus knew that Mary alone understood His mission.

A few moments of silence passed as she processed the staggering magnitude of this truth. It was at this point that Martha was simmering in the kitchen, agitated by her younger sister's ingratitude. How could Mary be so rude? The most prominent people in town would soon be at this dinner. Regardless of Martha's efficiency, there were countless things left to do in preparation. She and Lazarus had freely taken Mary in and forgiven her disgraceful past. The least her sister could do was show a little appreciation by helping in the kitchen!

Martha noticed the lull in their conversation and decided to protest her sister's lack of propriety. The agitated woman directed her remarks toward Jesus. If she couldn't get Mary to listen, surely her younger sister would obey Jesus.

"Lord . . ." Martha tapped her foot on the floor with her arms folded in irritation. "Do You not care that my sister has left me to serve alone? Therefore please tell her to help me" (Luke 10:40).

Jesus' reply was not what Martha expected. "Martha, Martha." His voice was filled with love and patient sympathy. "You are worried and troubled about many things. But one thing is needed, and Mary has chosen that good part, which will not be taken away from her" (verses 41, 42). At first stunned, Martha felt her face flare with embarrassment and shame. She too had wanted to sit as Mary did and commune with Jesus. She too had a thousand questions to ask of her gentle Guest, but fear that Jesus would see through her outer shell of composure and catch a glimpse of the severe loneliness within kept her aloof.

Martha's camouflage of constant activity kept her distracted from her own sins and heartache. Preoccupied with outward aesthetics, Martha didn't realize how much her sister required personal time with Jesus. Mary had been so easily overcome in the past, she desperately needed this instruction from Jesus to gain strength against temptation. Without another word Martha lowered her head and returned to her chores.

Her eyes fixed on Jesus, Mary gradually rose to her feet. Instead of moving toward the kitchen, she made for her own small room, where she retrieved her money bag and slipped out the front door. Mary understood from what Jesus said and the way He said it that she did not have much time left. She must find a gift fit for a king.

The Study

(Warning: Do not skip this next study! It may seem a bit deep, but it is essential to comprehending the essence of the gospel! Violators will be towed away at owner's expense!)

LUKE 10:38-42

"Now it happened as they went that He entered a certain village; and a certain woman named Martha welcomed Him into her house. And she had a sister called Mary, who also sat at Jesus' feet and heard His word. But Martha was distracted with much serving, and she approached Him and said, 'Lord, do You not care that my sister has left me to serve alone? Therefore tell her to help me.' And Jesus answered and said to her, 'Martha, Martha, you are worried and troubled about many things. But one thing is needed, and Mary has chosen that good part, which will not be taken away from her.'"

WORK FOR THE LORD

There are two basic and crucial issues in this passage. They must be examined in the proper order. One is "working for the Lord," and the other is "a relationship with the Lord." To confuse or misunderstand the rightful place of these two principles can be eternally devastating!

1. We do not work for the Lord *to be* saved or accepted. We work for Him because we *are* saved and because we *are* accepted.

2. We can be saved only through the relationship that grows from sitting at His feet and hearing the Word.

Martha was cumbered with much serving. But serving the Lord is never a substitute for really knowing Him. Jesus said in Matthew 7:22, 23: "Many will say to me in that day, Lord, Lord, have we not prophesied in thy name? and in thy name have cast out devils? and in thy name done many wonderful works? And then will I profess unto them, I never knew you: depart from me, ye that work iniquity" (KJV).

It is possible to do good works for Jesus without having a saving relationship with Him. The Lord warned that many will make the fatal mistake of thinking that good works guarantee salvation. Genuine service for God springs from a genuine knowledge of God. And this knowledge of God is the essence of salvation.

"This is eternal life, that they may know You, the only true God, and Jesus Christ whom You have sent" (John 17:3).

"My people are destroyed for lack of knowledge" (Hosea 4:6).

Once we really know God, the good works will follow. The Bible is clear that we are not saved *by* our works, but we will be judged and rewarded *according to* our works. "And the dead were judged according to their works, by the things which were written in the books" (Rev. 20:12). "And behold, I am coming quickly, and My reward is with Me, to give to every one according to his work" (Rev. 22:12).

Many will claim to know God, but their works will reveal a different story. "They profess to know God, but in works they deny Him, being abominable, disobedient, and disqualified for every good work" (Titus 1:16). "He who says, 'I know Him,' and does not keep His commandments, is a liar, and the truth is not in him" (1 John 2:4).

Jesus advised in Matthew 7:20: "Therefore by their fruits you will know them."

Mary had far more heart knowledge than head knowledge. Any Pharisee could have quickly bewildered her with doctrinal details, but when it came to knowing the Lord, Mary had her black belt.

DEVOTIONS

The importance of personal devotions and church attendance is often underestimated. It is possible to be so busy doing the work of the Lord that we forget the Lord of the work. Or, like Martha, become so busy working for the Lord, that we never really get to know Him.

Jesus established an order of priority between faith and works with His statement in Luke 10:41, 42: "Martha, Martha, you are worried and troubled about many things. But one thing is needed, and Mary has chosen that good part, which will not be taken away from her."

What was the "one thing" that Jesus was speaking about? It was the "one thing" He said the rich young ruler was lacking. "Then Jesus, looking at him, loved him, and said to him, 'One thing you lack'" (Mark 10:21).

It's the same one thing He always emphasized: Giving God first place; seeking a knowledge of the Lord that results in a saving faith. One thing is needed; without that "one thing" all the good works in the world cannot save a flea.

"But without faith it is impossible to please Him" (Heb. 11:6). "For by grace you have been saved through faith, and that not of yourselves; it is the gift of God, not of works, lest anyone should boast" (Eph. 2:8, 9).

Jesus said that the only good work that can save us is to believe in Him! "Jesus answered and said to them, 'This is the work of God, that you believe in Him whom He sent'" (John 6:29).

We are saved by faith in God, but real, saving faith in God will result only after we know God, and in turn trust Him.

Let me illustrate. If a total stranger walked up to me in the airport and handed me a check for $1 million, I would be more suspicious than happy. Not knowing the individual, I would question if this was a prank or a con. I might wonder if the person had just escaped from a mental institution. I would certainly have serious doubts about the value of the check. Why? Because I don't know the person. On the other hand, I have a few friends who are millionaires. Should one of them hand me a check for $1 million, I would be very, very excited. What's the difference? Knowing them gives me faith in their promises.

Likewise, faith in God follows knowing God. And how do I come to know God? Knowledge of and faith in God come primarily through reading His Word. "So then faith comes by hearing, and hearing by the word of God" (Rom. 10:17).

This simple sequence of three-point logic, if understood, changes lives.

1. We cannot obey the Lord unless we love Him. "If you love Me, keep My commandments" (John 14:15).

2. We cannot love the Lord unless we know Him.

3. And we cannot know the Lord unless we spend regular time with Him, at His feet, learning who He really is.

Every love relationship revolves around quality time, time spent communicating, talking, and listening. When we pray, we talk to God. When we read our Bibles or listen to the spoken Word, God talks to us. Hence, there is two-way communication.

THE WORD FIRST

As Mary found, sitting at Jesus' feet and hearing the Word becomes a priority for every Spirit-filled Christian. The apostles acted on this principle of priority when they ordained the seven deacons. "Then the twelve called the multitude of the disciples unto them, and said, It is not reason that we should leave the word of God, and serve tables. Wherefore, brethren, look ye out among you seven men of honest report, full of the Holy Ghost and wisdom, whom we may appoint over this business. But we will give ourselves continually to prayer, and to the ministry of the word" (Acts 6:2-4, KJV).

Simply put, the Word must be more important than the work. The work of the Lord will never flourish until the Word of the Lord has preeminence in the hearts of His people.

If a man has a heart attack and the paramedics arrive and begin by washing his face, filing his fingernails, and combing his hair instead of administrating CPR, he will probably die. Or, try to revive a dehydrated plant by wiping the dust off the leaves instead of watering its roots.

So many times I have sat on the platform during a church service or camp meeting, eagerly waiting to preach the Word, watching a seemingly endless parade of announcements, preliminaries, fanfare, and "special features" devour the precious time that should be dedicated to the proclamation of the Word. By the time I finally open my Bible to expound God's Word, many in the congregation are restless and irritable, already eyeing their watches, ready to leave. Other people, suffering from low blood sugar, are unable to comprehend what I am saying anyway. The Lord is given our mental leftovers, a lame offering of our attention.

As important as they are, church announcements, special music, baby dedications, yes, even baptisms and the Communion service, should never replace or eclipse the reading of the sacred Word.

MANNA IN THE MORNING

Morning is the best time for getting to know God. This principle was deeply impressed upon the children of Israel by His daily gift of manna. The angel food cake rained down from heaven early in the morning, six days a week, for 40 years. If one waited too long to gather it, the manna would evaporate in the heat of the desert sun. "And they gathered it every morning, every man according to his eating: and when the sun waxed hot, it melted" (Ex. 16:21, KJV).

Likewise, if we wait too long for our spiritual devotions, the cares and pressures of the day will get our attention before the Lord does. The busier we are and the more we have to do, the more we need to take time to pray. Let's not allow the manna to melt.

Jesus, our example, practiced morning devotions. "And in the morning, rising up a great while before day, he went out, and departed into a solitary place, and there prayed" (Mark 1:35, KJV).

As famous evangelist Charles Spurgeon well said: "The morning is the gate of the day, and it should be well guarded with prayer. It is one end of the thread on which the day's actions are strung, and should be well knotted with devotion. If we felt the majesty of life we should be more careful of its mornings.

"He who rushes from his bed to his business and waiteth not to worship is as foolish as though he had not put on his clothes, or cleansed his face, and as unwise as though he had dashed into battle without arms or armor. Be it ours to bathe in the softly flowing river of communion with God, before the heat of the wilderness and the burden of the day begins to oppress."

BIBLE BREAD

Spiritual food is just as essential as physical food. If we are late for work and must choose between a bowl of raisin bran or personal devotions, many might feel their quiet time with God is expendable. As important as fiber may be to our well-being, it will not keep us from sin when temptation comes.

"I have esteemed the words of his mouth more than my necessary food" (Job 23:12, KJV). "Thy words were found, and I did eat them" (Jer. 15:16, KJV). When we pray "Give us this day our daily bread," it applies more to the spiritual bread than the baked variety (Matt. 6:11). When Jesus was tempted in the wilderness after a 40-day fast, He told the devil, "It is written, That man shall not live by bread alone, but by every word of God" (Luke 4:4, KJV).

We cannot depend on others to feed us spiritually. Mature Christians must learn to bake their own "Bible bread."

If you've ever visited Yellowstone National Park, you were probably given a piece of paper by a ranger at the park entrance. Printed in big letters was the warning "Do Not Feed the Bears." But no sooner did you drive into the heart of the park than you saw people everywhere feeding the bears.

A tourist asked a park ranger, "Why bother with the warnings and the road signs?" The ranger answered, "The tourists have only a small part of the picture." He told how, in winter, the park service personnel must drive around the park with a backhoe to carry away the frozen bodies of dead bears—bears who have starved because they couldn't feed themselves. They had become so used to dining on the doughnuts and goodies offered by well-meaning tourists that they had lost the ability to hunt real food as the Creator designed. When the park closed for the winter and they were left to their own devisings, they starved to death.

POWER FOOD

I can't explain it, but spiritual food seemed to give Jesus not only spiritual strength but physical strength as well. John 4:31, 32 says, "In the mean while his disciples prayed him, saying, Master, eat. But he said unto them, I have meat to eat that ye know not of" (KJV).

Elijah received supernatural physical strength from eating the heavenly bread an angel prepared. "And the angel of the Lord came again the second time, and touched him, and said, Arise and eat; because the journey is too great for thee. And he arose, and did eat and drink, and went in the strength of that meat forty days and forty nights unto Horeb the mount of God" (1 Kings 19:7, 8, KJV).

By awakening a little earlier to have more devotional time with God, you may find that you have increased physical and mental energy throughout the day as well. To resist the daily temptations that assail us, we need the same secret weapon Jesus used. It is described in Ephesians 6:17: "Take . . . the sword of the Spirit, which is the word of God."

JESUS IN ME

A mother and her 3-year-old daughter were riding in a car when suddenly the little girl put her head on her mother's chest and began to listen.

"What are you doing?" Mom asked.

"I'm listening for Jesus in your heart" was the reply.

"Well, what do you hear?"

The innocent child looked up with a look of perplexity in her eyes and said, "Sounds to me like He's making coffee!"

Christians not only have the promise that Jesus will be with us to the end (Matt. 28:20), but He wants to abide in us as well. How do we avail ourselves of this promise? "Thy word have I hid in mine heart, that I might not sin against thee" (Ps. 119:11, KJV). Inasmuch as Jesus is the Word, it would be safe to say that Jesus Himself is the secret weapon! When we spend more time with Jesus through prayer and Bible study, we will know Him better and therefore love Him more. He will abide in our thoughts and heart. Just as our natural reaction is to talk about those we love, so it will become more natural for us to talk to others about our Lord. As a muscle is strengthened by activity, so when we share Jesus with others our own faith will become stronger.

More love, more witnessing, more surrender, more energy equal less discouragement and less depression. All this is a direct chain reaction that comes from using the secret weapon of personal devotions.

All of us desperately need and want Jesus abiding in our hearts. How do we get Him there? Since another name for Jesus is the Word, in reading the Word we are directly inviting Jesus into our hearts and minds and lives: "Christ in you, the hope of glory" (Col. 1:27).

Biblically illiterate

One of the single most important things we can do to experience a personal and corporate revival in our lives is to hear the Word. But in recent years I have become increasingly alarmed at the appalling ignorance of Scripture I have observed in the churches and Christian schools I have visited.

The following is a list of some of the more humorous answers given by students regarding basic Bible questions:

1. Lot's wife was a pillar of salt by day and a ball of fire by night.

2. Moses went to the top of Mount Cyanide to get the Ten Commandments.

3. The seventh commandment is "Thou shalt not admit adultery."

4. Joshua led the Hebrews in the battle of Geritol.

5. Jesus was born because Mary had an immaculate contraption.

6. The people who followed Jesus were called the 12 decibels.

7. The epistles were the wives of the apostles.

8. One of the opossums was Saint Matthew.

9. David fought the Frankinsteins, a race of people who lived in biblical times.

10. A Christian should have only one wife. This is called holy monotony.

Unfortunately these comical responses from the children reflect a serious intrinsic spiritual famine among the adults.

Spiritual and physical laws

Early in my Christian experience I met a man who firmly impressed upon my mind this truth. One day as I walked down the street I heard his three-wheeled bicycle squeak up behind me. Among the young people in Palm Springs, California, Brother Harold was a living legend, a 70-year-old Jewish Christian who knew how to "walk the talk."

Brother Harold's day began at 4:00 a.m. with two hours of Bible study and prayer, followed by a few hours on the street handing out tracts. After that he was off to the hospital, where he served as a self-appointed chaplain. He would visit patients in their rooms and share an encouraging scripture or two, all from memory. I will never forget how his voice quivered with joy and his face shone whenever he quoted the Bible.

I was a new convert, about 17, and struggling to separate my former hippie, Eastern philosophy from the truths of the Bible. Actually, I was feeling a bit like a failure as a Christian.

Brother Harold met me that morning with "What a glorious day God has given us." (Brother Harold was always so "up.")

"Yeah, nice day," I responded.

He detected something missing from my voice. "How long can you hold your breath, Doug?" Brother Harold asked with a twinkle in his eye.

What a strange question. I remembered playing a little game in school, holding my breath while waiting for the bell to ring. I had become pretty good at it.

I laughed at his "left field" question. "I can hold my breath for four minutes if I hyperventilate first."

"Then, son, you should not go any longer than four minutes without praying," he quipped. " 'Pray without ceasing.' First Thessalonians 5:17." His voice quivered with deep reverence for the Scriptures.

"How often do you eat?" he asked next.

Now I understood where he was heading. "About two or three times a day," I slowly answered.

"Well, that's how often you should read or meditate on God's Word." He paused for a moment, then continued. "Doug, what would happen to your body if you never exercised?"

"I guess I would get weak and flabby."

"Same thing happens to your faith if you don't use it," he said.

As he pedaled his bike away he called over his shoulder, "The same laws that apply to your physical body also apply to your spiritual health."

I knew Brother Harold had just put his finger on my greatest need. I was neglecting to sit, like Mary, at Jesus' feet and hear the Word. The Word of God is our bread to nourish, our sword to defend and conquer, and the light to guide us to glory.

CHAPTER FOUR

SIMON'S FEAST

The Story

After leaving Martha's house, Mary hurried the two miles into Jerusalem to a street where the finer shops were located. She had become so absorbed in finding the perfect gift for Jesus that it only now occurred to her that this was her first return to the holy city since that extraordinary day when Jesus had saved her from being stoned to death.

Just as Mary was pondering this thought, she saw one of her former clients, a lawyer. The attorney was walking slowly down the narrow street in her direction. The man was evidently being towed along, like an ox with a ring in his nose, by his wife, who was leisurely shopping. A moment of panic seized Mary as memories of her sordid past flooded through her mind. Before she could duck into one of the shops, the lawyer looked right at her without the slightest indication that he recognized her.

That's when it occurred to Mary that she no longer wore the paint and seductive trappings of a prostitute. Yet there was something more. Mary was different on the inside as well. Friends and family had commented that since she had become a disciple of Jesus she glowed with an inner light.

Overwhelmed by a fresh appreciation for Jesus and all He had done for her, Mary redirected her attention to finding a worthy gift for the Master. If necessary, she would empty her purse to pay for it. The money she had saved from her former life and from selling her place in Magdala amounted to a substantial sum, but it was a constant reminder of the wages of sin. Mary determined to spend all of it that day, if necessary, in purchasing a noble present as an offering to the Lord.

As the former prostitute examined a rack of fine purple cloth, she became aware of a rich and rare fragrance permeating the air and gently caressing her senses. It came from the apothecary shop across the narrow cobblestone street. She released the royal-purple fabric and drifted to the spot where the perfumer was pouring the last few drops of the enchanting essence from a mixing bowl into a beautiful, ornate, white alabaster flask. The rare and pleasing aroma drew other shoppers and Passover pilgrims to the shop entrance like bees to a nectar-laden flower.

"What is that incredible perfume?" one of the female shoppers asked with a sound of awe and reverence in her voice.

"This, my dear"—the shop owner held up the exquisite bottle for all to see—"is my own special mixture of spikenard and myrrh. I concocted the formula from the one described in the Song of Solomon."

He waxed eloquent to the gathering crowd of shoppers. "Only once a year the caravans from Sheba bring me enough of the right materials to fill a single flask. In fact"—he paused and the crowd leaned forward to hear his suddenly secretive message—"last year Pilate purchased my flask and sent it as a gift to Caesar. But this year's mixture," the man paused again, holding up the beautiful engraved jar, "is my best ever!"

Oohs and aahs rippled through the growing crowd. Feeling as if she were being pushed by angels, Mary pressed her way forward and asked, "How much does it cost?"

The man eyed the slender young woman dressed in common clothes and chuckled. "Young lady, it would take a year's wages to buy a gift like this!"

Mary held up her money bag for him to see and asked again, "How much?"

The perfume specialist's eyes narrowed greedily at the bulging leather sack. His expression grew more serious. After thinking for a moment, he announced, "Three hundred fifty denarii."

The crowd gasped at the steep price for the perfume.

Mary sighed, then smiled sweetly. She was accustomed to dickering with greedy men. "I have 300 denarii. You can make an immediate sale!"

The merchant was stunned that a woman of her demeanor would be carrying so much, but he held his ground. "I'm sorry, dear woman," he said, "but I make only one of these a year and . . ."

Mary didn't want to hear his explanation. "This is to be a gift for Jesus of Nazareth."

The man stepped back and studied Mary's face thoughtfully for a minute. The crowd pressed closer to hear his reply.

"Did you say Jesus of Nazareth?"

Mary nodded.

A man in the crowd blurted out, "Many say He is the son of David and will reign as our new king."

There was a long pause as the bystanders became emotionally involved in the negotiations and watched the shop owner's face. Then his eyes twinkled, and the wizard of perfumes and ointments smiled at Mary and said, "All right. It will be an honor to sell you my perfume for 300 denarii to anoint our new king."

The crowd applauded in approval. Fearful that the perfume chemist might change his mind, Mary quickly emptied the contents of her purse onto his workbench. Before he could finish counting the money she scooped up the beautiful, newly sealed flask, closed her eyes, and inhaled the lingering fragrance.

"Thank you," she breathed as the awed crowd of shoppers cleared a pathway for her. "And may the Lord bless you," she called over her shoulder.

"Shalom," the apothecary merchant replied.

Mary hurried toward home, carefully cradling her new acquisition with both hands. When she arrived at Martha and Lazarus' home in Bethany, everyone had already left for Uncle Simon's house. Quickly changing into a clean dress, she placed the white alabaster flask in her bag and headed out the door. At the doorstep she paused thoughtfully, then returned to her room to retrieve her other most precious possession. Soon her feet flew over the cobblestone streets to Simon's house.

The hour for the much-celebrated feast had come. The entire village was buzzing with excitement. Throughout the afternoon, curious onlookers lingered near the entrance to Uncle Simon's courtyard, hoping to get a glimpse of the Man who could raise the dead and heal lepers.

Because of the publicity already connected with the upcoming dinner, Jesus had chosen to retreat to the Garden of Gethsemane for some quiet time with His disciples. An atmosphere of solemn intensity had surrounded Jesus during the past few days. He seemed eager to seize every opportunity to be alone with the 12, to instruct them in the code of His kingdom.

Even the disciples sensed that something monumental was about to transpire. Secretly they hoped that Jesus was about to make His move and use His supernatural powers to overthrow the Roman Empire and seat Himself on David's throne. What better time than the Passover week to establish His new kingdom, they reasoned, when tens of thousands of loyal Jewish pilgrims would be in Jerusalem to join the ranks of the new army?

The topic of Jesus' earthly rule always led the disciples into emotional discussions regarding who should hold the highest positions of the new government. The only thing they could ever agree upon was that Judas should be the treasurer in the new cabinet.

Judas had a more formal education than the other disciples and was therefore highly respected by his peers. He had been a scribe, who, after witnessing one of Jesus' miracles of healing, approached the Master and said, "Teacher, I will follow You wherever You go."

They'd all been surprised when Jesus, as if cautioning him against false hopes for worldly gain, said, "Foxes have holes and birds of the air have nests, but the Son of Man has nowhere to lay His head" (Luke 9:58). Despite the cryptic answer, Judas' ambition compelled him to follow the Teacher. Clever, Judas made it a point to maneuver himself quietly so as to be near the Lord until he was considered one of Jesus' disciples. It wasn't long after the former scribe joined the group that the other 11 voted he should carry their meager money purse.

But Judas made Mary uncomfortable. If nothing else, the former prostitute knew how to read deceptive men. She discerned something devious about his conduct. Judas sensed that she could read him and was, therefore, never overly kind to Mary.

Of all Jesus' disciples, Matthew was the most sensitive and understanding of the woman. He himself, a former publican, knew what it was like to be one of society's outcasts. He could identify with Mary's appreciation for Jesus' mercy.

When Mary arrived at the feast, Martha had just finished seating Jesus and the guests in Simon's courtyard. She could tell that Judas was obviously insulted that Jesus, Lazarus, and Simon were at the head of the table, while he had been seated at the foot with some of the less notable guests. Even John, the youngest of the group, was nearer the head of the table. Mary could sense that Judas was trying, unsuccessfully, to hide his offended pride. Yet it didn't take much to see that the man was indignant and brooding.

Then Jesus, observing how Judas and some of the guests vied for the best places at the tables, gave a little homily. "When you are invited by anyone to a wedding feast, do not sit down in the best place, lest one more honorable than you be invited by him; and he who invited you and him come and say to you, 'Give place to this man,' and then you begin with shame to take the lowest place.

"But when you are invited, go and sit down in the lowest place, so that when he who invited you comes he may say to you, 'Friend, go up higher.' Then you will have glory in the presence of those who sit at the table with you. For whoever exalts himself will be humbled, and he who humbles himself will be exalted" (Luke 14:8-11).

Even though Jesus gave this subtle rebuke in a general format, Judas' face reddened, revealing he'd felt the sting. He believed he had been singled out and had now become even more incensed.

Meanwhile Mary, anxiously watching for a moment alone with Jesus so as to give Him her present, realized that if she was going to make the presentation before His enemies arrested Him she would have to act soon. And yet Mary knew that presenting her gift at this very public event could cause a spectacle and might definitely be misunderstood. While she was pondering what she should do, Jesus began to share another lesson.

This time Jesus directed His comments to Simon: "When you give a dinner or a supper, do not ask your friends, your brothers, your relatives, nor rich neighbors, lest they also invite you back, and you be repaid. But when you give a feast, invite the poor, the maimed, the lame, the blind. And you will be blessed, because they cannot repay you; for you shall be repaid at the resurrection of the just" (verses 12-14).

When one of the scribes who sat at the table with Him heard these things, he said with a pious air, "Blessed is he who shall eat bread in the kingdom of God!" (verse 15). Then Jesus said to him, "A certain man gave a great supper and invited many, and sent his servant at supper time to say to those who were invited, 'Come, for all things are now ready.'

"But they all with one accord began to make excuses. The first said to him, 'I have bought a piece of ground, and I must go and see it. I ask you to have me excused.' And another said, 'I have bought five yoke of oxen, and I am going to test them. I ask you to have me excused.'

"Still another said, 'I have married a wife, and therefore I cannot come.'

"So that servant came and reported these things to his master. Then the master of the house, being angry, said to his servant, 'Go out quickly into the streets and lanes of the city, and bring in here the poor and the maimed and the lame and the blind.' And the servant said, 'Master, it is done as you commanded, and still there is room.' Then the master said to the servant, 'Go out into the highways and hedges, and compel them to come in, that my house may be filled. For I say to you that none of those men who were invited shall taste my supper'" (verses 16-24).

An awkward silence followed this parable, as if Jesus had unveiled the selfish attitudes of many of the guests. But this last story made Mary feel a sense of urgency. If she did not act now, opportunity to demonstrate her love for the Lord might never come again. It was now or never. Her courageous heart pounded; her palms sweated.

Simon had spared no expense on this event. He would serve only the best. The guests were in reclining positions and leaning against dining cushions, with their legs stretched outward away from the table. They sat slightly elevated so that a servant could wash their feet before the food was served.

Martha directed a constant flow of servants carrying a luscious assortment of food on silver trays. Mary sidled up to her sister. "Why hasn't Uncle Simon first washed the feet of his guests?"

Distracted, Martha glared at Mary. "Where did you go? You never did help me prepare for this event, and now you point out the one thing we overlooked." Martha rolled her eyes toward the ceiling, then added, "Simon neglected to provide the basins and towels. What was I supposed to do?"

Notwithstanding Simon's social gaffe, everyone seemed to be enjoying the fine cuisine and the animated conversation. "I could certainly have used your help this afternoon," the older sister repeated. Spying a servant carrying a tray of less-than-perfect baked barley cakes wrapped in grape leaves, Martha rushed to stop the man from serving the damaged food. Mary watched her sister hustle the servant back into the kitchen.

Because all eyes were fixed on Jesus as He spoke, no one noticed when Mary softly slipped into the room and knelt quietly by the Master's feet. She had been breathless with fear, but now, kneeling at His feet, a familiar peace settled over her. She sensed she was safe, under the everlasting wings of the Almighty. She silently prayed that Jesus would approve her deed of love. What the others thought was of no consequence to her.

Then, with loving tenderness, she broke the seal on the alabaster flask and poured some of the contents of precious oil liberally over Jesus' feet. Jesus did not even flinch. He simply paused in His discourse, smiled to acknowledge to Mary that He was aware of her act of service and sacrifice, then continued His conversation.

As the fragrant oil ran down Jesus' feet, a drop spilled on the tile floor. Realizing that in her haste she had forgotten to bring a cloth or towel to spread the ointment evenly, without a second thought Mary removed the shawl covering her head and released her long, luxuriously rich brown hair. She began wiping Jesus' feet, spreading the oil with her hair.

Tears of gratitude and love flowed freely down her cheeks, spilling onto His feet and coalescing with the ointment. When she saw her tears shining on Jesus' feet, she remembered her other most precious possession. Drawing out the glass tear vial from a pouch in her robe, she removed the wax cap and proceeded to clean His feet with her tears and dry them with her hair.

Mary was so absorbed, lost in the joy of serving Jesus, that she was oblivious to the stunned reactions of the guests around the table. Soon after she broke open the alabaster flask the room filled with the profusion of costly, exotic essence. The conversation in the room quieted to a tense murmur. Even the servants froze, not certain what they should do about the situation.

Mary now felt the piercing stares of all present. Fearing someone might try to prohibit her from completing her mission, she resolutely stood and poured the remaining oil on Jesus' head, amid gasps of astonishment and shock. Her act, though unpremeditated, was the traditional symbol among the Jews for the sealing and anointing of a new king or priest.

Judas, pretending to be indignant, protested under his breath, just loud enough for those seated nearby to hear. "What a tragic waste of resources! Why, this oil could have been sold for more than 300 denarii." Then as an afterthought to cloak his own greedy designs, he added, "Of course, the proceeds could have been donated to the poor!"

Some of the other disciples nodded in agreement. What Judas' peers didn't know was that his selfish heart had felt keenly rebuked by Mary's liberal generosity.

Jesus heard His faithful disciples echo Judas' murmurings. With sad compassion He said to them, "Why do you trouble the woman? For she has done a good work for Me. For you have the poor with you always, but Me, you do not have always. For in pouring this fragrant oil on My body, she did it for My burial" (Matt. 26:10-12).

This clear statement of Jesus' approval brought ecstatic joy to Mary's heart. Knowing that Jesus was pleased with her was all she ever wanted. The weeping woman fell again to her knees and resumed kissing His feet.

Judas turned red with resentment. It was bad enough that he had been seated at the foot of the table, but now Jesus was openly rebuking him in front of his peers. If Jesus did not appreciate his wisdom and talents, Judas knew someone who would. From the supper he went to the priests, to trade the Saviour of the world for common silver.

Simon, on the other hand, was not so much offended by Mary's gift as by the giver herself. He knew all too well about Mary's soiled past, and he was shocked that Jesus would let a woman with her reputation touch Him. Most religious leaders would not permit so much as the shadow of a publican or prostitute to touch them in public for fear of losing the respect of the people.

Simon tightened his lips and furrowed his brow. "This man," Simon thought within himself, "if He were a prophet, would know who and what manner of woman this is who is touching Him, for she is a sinner" (Luke 7:39).

Jesus broke the awkward silence and answered Simon's thoughts: "Simon, I have something to say to you" (verse 40).

Simon replied, "Teacher, say it" (verse 40).

"There was a certain creditor who had two debtors. One owed five hundred denarii, and the other fifty. And when they had nothing with which to repay, he freely forgave them both. Tell Me, therefore, which of them will love him more?" (verses 41, 42).

Simon answered, "I suppose the one whom he forgave more" (verse 43).

And Jesus replied, "You have rightly judged" (verse 43).

Jesus looked at the woman, then back at Simon. "Do you see this woman? I entered your house; you gave Me no water for My feet, but she has washed My feet with her tears and wiped them with the hair of her head.

"You gave Me no kiss, but this woman has not ceased to kiss My feet since the time I came in. You did not anoint My head with oil, but this woman has anointed My feet with fragrant oil. Therefore I say to you, her sins, which are many, are forgiven, for she loved much. But to whom little is forgiven, the same loves little" (verses 44–47).

Rather than grow angry with Jesus as did Judas, Simon's eyes grew moist with regret. He had forgotten so quickly how much he had been forgiven when Jesus healed him of his leprosy. No sooner had the visible evidence of his leprosy faded than he quickly slipped back into his self-righteous role, forgetting that he was as big a sinner as Mary.

Then to remove any doubts regarding the main purpose of His mission, Jesus turned to Mary and said, "Your sins are forgiven" (verse 48). Jesus' words were like heavenly music to her ears. Mary prostrated herself at His feet in a posture of abject worship as the last lingering drops of guilt and shame evaporated from her soul in the warm glow of His forgiveness.

Though Mary was oblivious to the stares of the other guests, she clearly heard their muffled tones. "Who is this who even forgives sins?" (verse 49).

But to Mary, having the approval of Jesus was all that mattered. She was already satisfied with His approbation, but to remove any lingering question that she would be accepted among His disciples He added, "Assuredly, I say to you, wherever this gospel is preached in the whole world, what this woman has done will also be told as a memorial to her" (Matt. 26:13).

Then Jesus gently placed His hand on her head and blessed her. "Your faith has saved you. Go in peace" (Luke 7:50).

The Study

JOHN 12:1-3, KJV

"Then Jesus six days before the passover came to Bethany, where Lazarus was which had been dead, whom he raised from the dead. There they made him a supper; and Martha served: but Lazarus was one of them that sat at the table with him. Then took Mary a pound of ointment of spikenard, very costly, and anointed the feet of Jesus, and wiped his feet with her hair: and the house was filled with the odour of the ointment."

MARK 14:3, KJV

"And being in Bethany in the house of Simon the leper, as he sat at meat, there came a woman having an alabaster box of ointment of spikenard very precious; and she brake the box, and poured it on his head."

IT COSTS HOW MUCH?

Mary at Jesus' feet in sacrifice and service was in many respects at her finest. This is evident by the fact that Jesus would immortalize the deed by declaring, "Wherever this gospel is preached in the whole world, what this woman has done will also be told as a memorial to her" (Matt. 26:13). Why? Because Mary gave her all!

It may sound radical or even scary, but if you would be saved, it will require your all. A total surrender, a total sacrifice. This is the same reason that Jesus commended the widow who cast her last two coins into the offering box—she gave her all: "And he saw also a certain poor widow casting in thither two mites. And he said, Of a truth I say unto you, that this poor widow hath cast in more than they all: For all these have of their abundance cast in unto the offerings of God: but she of her penury hath cast in all the living that she had" (Luke 21:2-4, KJV).

Many never experience the fullness of God's peace and power, because they make only a partial surrender. The Lord can fill our vessels only to the extent that we empty them.

"For whoever desires to save his life will lose it, but whoever loses his life for My sake will find it" (Matt. 16:25).

"Again, the kingdom of heaven is like treasure hidden in a field, which a man found and hid; and for joy over it he goes and sells all that he has and buys that field. Again, the kingdom of heaven is like a merchant seeking beautiful pearls, who, when he had found one pearl of great price, went and sold all that he had and bought it" (Matt. 13:44-46).

When the rich young ruler asked Jesus what he had to do to acquire eternal life Jesus said to him, " 'If you want to be perfect, go, sell what you have and give to the poor, and you will have treasure in heaven; and come, follow Me.' But when the young man heard that saying, he went away sorrowful, for he had great possessions" (Matt. 19:21, 22).

How tragic that this young man went away with great possessions and sorrow. Millions the world over are making the same bad choice, striving to find happiness through materialism and money. This is why Jesus next warned, "Assuredly, I say to you that it is hard for a rich man to enter the kingdom of heaven" (verse 23).

And again He cautioned them, "Take heed and beware of covetousness, for one's life does not consist in the abundance of the things he possesses" (Luke 12:15). "For what profit is it to a man if he gains the whole world, and loses his own soul?" (Matt. 16:26).

Right after filling their nets to bursting, the most prosperous catch of their lives, Jesus asked Peter, Andrew, James, and John to leave it all and follow Him. And they did! "So when they had brought their boats to land, they forsook all and followed Him" (Luke 5:11). "Then Peter said, Lo, we have left all, and followed thee" (Luke 18:28, KJV).

Is the Lord asking all of us to liquidate all our assets and follow Him? Not necessarily, but He is asking us to put everything on the altar and be willing to do whatever He directs. He is asking for all of our hearts; then He will naturally have everything else of us.

"Jesus said to him, 'You shall love the Lord your God with all your heart, with all your soul, and with all your mind' " (Matt 22:37).

LET GO AND LET GOD

It has been told that monkey trappers in North Africa have a clever method of catching their prey. A number of gourds are filled with nuts and firmly chained to a tree. Each gourd has a hole just large enough for the unsuspecting monkey to stick its hand through. When a hungry or curious animal discovers this treasure of nuts, it reaches in and grabs a handful. But the hole is too small for it to withdraw its bulging fist. It doesn't have enough sense to open its hand and release the deceptive booty, so it is easily taken captive.

This is a fitting picture of many Christians. The devil traps them with his crafty snares; he appeals to their natural greed and carnal appetites, which lead to their spiritual downfall. As long as they hold on to this worldly bait, they cannot escape from Satan's trap. But he keeps on urging, "Don't let go!" Listening to the tempter's alluring voice, they vainly continue to attempt escape, without letting go of the world. It is impossible to "let God" until we first "let go" of everything and everyone! That's right—not even people must take priority over our relationship with God! That's why the first and great commandment is to love God with all our heart; then secondarily, to love our neighbor as ourselves.

"He who loves father or mother more than Me is not worthy of Me. And he who loves son or daughter more than Me is not worthy of Me" (Matt. 10:37).

The good news is that whoever has the faith to trust God and surrender all for Christ's sake will be abundantly compensated in this life and the next.

"So Jesus answered and said, 'Assuredly, I say to you, there is no one who has left house or brothers or sisters or father or mother or wife or children or lands, for My sake and the gospel's, who shall not receive a hundredfold now in this time—houses and brothers and sisters and mothers and children and lands, with persecutions—and in the age to come, eternal life" (Mark 10:29, 30).

LOVE GIVES LAVISHLY

I know a man, a fairly prosperous businessman, whose son was convicted of murder and sentenced to life in prison. The loving father, convinced that his son was innocent, mortgaged his home and sold all the family's assets to pay the legal fees to get his son another trial. Even though the conviction stood, the father never regretted the sacrifice. Why did he do it? Love gives sacrificially. You know this one: "For God so loved the world that He gave!" God the Father gave His all when He sent His only beloved Son.

When Naaman the Syrian was healed from his leprosy, his first reaction was to give something to Elisha the prophet, not to pay for his cleansing, but from a sense of profound thanks (2 Kings 5). His lavish offering was in proportion to his great gratitude. After Zacchaeus was forgiven by Christ his response was to give abundantly (Luke 19:1-10).

Mary, too, felt called upon to give to her Saviour out of overflowing gratitude, because she appreciated how much she had been forgiven.

"Therefore I say to you, her sins, which are many, are forgiven, for she loved much. But to whom little is forgiven, the same loves little" (Luke 7:47). It is also safe to say, he who has a concept of how much he has been forgiven will love much. This is why Mary gave lavishly in ministering to Jesus. "And certain women who had been healed of evil spirits and infirmities—Mary called Magdalene, out of whom had come seven demons, and Joanna the wife of Chuza, Herod's steward, and Susanna, and many others who provided for Him from their substance" (Luke 8:2, 3).

Then near the end of His life Mary gave totally for the crisis when she bought the alabaster perfume.

"So let each one give as he purposes in his heart, not grudgingly or of necessity; for God loves a cheerful giver" (2 Cor. 9:7).

THE ANOINTED

From ancient times, priests and kings were ceremonially anointed with oil as a sign of official appointment to office, and as a symbol of God's Spirit and power upon them. "And he poured some of the anointing oil on Aaron's head and anointed him, to consecrate him" (Lev. 8:12). Another example of this is Captain Jehu's being anointed with a box of oil by one of the prophets to seal his appointment as king: "Then take the box of oil, and pour it on his head, and say, Thus saith the Lord, I have anointed thee king over Israel" (2 Kings 9:3, KJV).

This points up the tremendous significance of Mary's anointment of the Lord just before the cross—Jesus was being sealed as our King, Priest, and Sacrifice!

The Hebrew *mashach,* or "messiah," and the Greek *Christos* are both translated "anointed one." Some people think Christ was the last name of Jesus, but the word "Christ" is a title: "the anointed one."

Mary's washing or anointing Jesus' feet with her tears was significant of Jesus walking in our sorrows and feeling our pain. "You number my wanderings; put my tears into Your bottle; are they not in Your book?" (Ps. 56:8). Our feet were bathed in His tears, and His head was crowned with the thorns of our sins. This is why the prophet said, "Surely He has borne our griefs and carried our sorrows" (Isa. 53:4).

HUMBLE SERVICE

A hospital visitor once saw a nurse tending to the ugly sores of a leprosy patient and said, "I'd never do that for a million dollars!"

The nurse answered, "Neither would I. But I do it for Jesus for nothing." Genuine love is willing to serve without any recognition or even remuneration.

How do you spell success? In the world, success often is defined by what kind of car a person drives, what kind of clothes are worn, what kind of house a family owns. With the Lord it's not what kind of car the person drives but what kind of person drives the car. With Him the issue is what kind of woman wears the dress and what kind of family lives in the house. People look on the outward appearances, while God looks on the heart. With God success is not defined by how much you have but how much you give. Do people fear you or love you? In the world, greatness is measured by how many people work for you, but God looks to see how many people you serve.

Napoleon Bonaparte said, "Alexander, Caesar, Charlemagne, and myself founded empires; but upon what did we rest the creations of our genius? Upon force. Jesus Christ alone founded His empire upon love, and at this hour millions of men would die for Him."

The Bible teaches that a woman's hair is her glory (1 Cor. 11:15). The visual message in Mary's act of wiping His feet with her hair was one of totally humble service, submission, worship, and surrender. "Jesus met them, saying, 'Rejoice!' So they came and held Him by the feet and worshiped Him" (Matt. 28:9).

F. B. Meyer once said, "I used to think that God's gifts were on shelves one above the other, and that the taller we grew in Christian character the easier we could reach them. I now find that God's gifts are on shelves one beneath the other. It is not a question of growing taller but of stooping lower; that we have to go down, always down, to get His best gifts."

JUDAS

"Then one of His disciples, Judas Iscariot, Simon's son, who would betray Him, said, 'Why was this fragrant oil not sold for three hundred denarii and given to the poor?' This he said, not that he cared for the poor, but because he was a thief, and had the money box; and he used to take what was put in it" (John 12:4-6).

Two people in Scripture are recorded as kissing Jesus: Judas kissed His face, then betrayed Him. Mary kissed His feet, then served Him. The genuine sacrifice and service of Mary was a stinging rebuke to the selfishness of Judas.

It is often true that those who, like Judas, look down their noses at sinful Mary are doing it as a diversionary tactic lest someone focus on their sins (John 12:7). The most critical and judgmental people in the church are usually the ones who are struggling with their own hidden guilt. It was immediately after Judas' pious statement of concern for the poor that he went out and agreed to betray the Saviour for the price of a slave.

A PUBLIC DISPLAY

Mary was not ashamed to make a spectacle of herself in showing her love for Jesus. But many Christians are afraid to show their love for Jesus publicly, in the workplace or neighborhood, for fear of being ridiculed for their faith. I have observed that many Christians, when they eat in a public restaurant, wait until they think no one is looking, then quickly bow their heads for three seconds to thank God silently for their food.

"For whoever is ashamed of Me and My words, of him the Son of Man will be ashamed when He comes in His own glory, and in His Father's, and of the holy angels" (Luke 9:26).

Because Mary was not afraid to openly demonstrate her loyalty and submission to Jesus, the Lord was willing to defend her in public. "Therefore the Lord God of Israel says: . . . 'Those who honor Me I will honor, and those who despise Me shall be lightly esteemed'" (1 Sam. 2:30).

That's why Jesus said of Mary, "Let her alone"; He was very protective of Mary because He understood her heart. Remember, the Lord even had a few adulterers and recovered prostitutes in His family tree—Rahab, Tamar, Bathsheba. In fact, His own mother's reputation had been besmirched by the circumstances around His unusual conception. Also remember, Mary is a symbol of the church, and, flawed and defective though she may appear, Jesus is grieved and angered by those who, like Judas, stand by and accuse the bride of Christ.

The Presbyterian minister Robert Falconer was witnessing among a destitute people in a certain foreign city. He read to them this story of how Mary Magdalene washed Jesus' feet with her tears and dried them with her hair. While he was reading he heard a loud sob and looked up at a young, thin girl whose face was disfigured by smallpox. After he spoke a few words of encouragement to her, she asked, "Will He ever come again, the One who forgave the woman? I have heard that He will come again. Will it be soon?" Falconer assured her He would return someday soon. After sobbing again uncontrollably, she said, "Sir, can't He wait a little while? My hair ain't long enough yet to wipe His feet."

When we begin to see how much Jesus suffered and paid for our sins, when we are genuinely converted from our selfish striving for recognition and grasping for earthly gain, then and only then will we be truly content to humbly serve and give all to the One who gave all.

CHAPTER
AT THE CROSS
FIVE

The Story

O nly a few days had passed since the memorable dinner at Simon's house, and now Mary, Martha, and Lazarus sat to- gether for another special meal. An awful sense of foreboding hung over the small band of disciples in Bethany as they ate the simple Passover fare that Thursday evening. Mary keenly felt the awkward silence. Somehow it seemed like a farewell gesture when Jesus announced that this year He would eat in the holy city with the 12. Everyone knew about the growing number of enemies in Jerusalem who were plotting for Jesus' life. Only a few days earlier the priest and scribes became infuriated when a vast multitude hailed Him as the "Son of David," saying "Blessed is He who comes in the name of the Lord! Hosanna in the highest!" (Matt. 21:9).

Jesus had ridden on the back of a borrowed donkey colt that had never had a rider down the slope of Mount Olivet, through the Beautiful Gate, to the Temple. Every Jew understood the profound significance of this act. The Master was living out one of the most well-known prophecies regarding the coming of the Messiah.

"Rejoice greatly, O daughter of Zion! Shout, O daughter of Jerusalem! Behold, your King is coming to you; He is just and hav- ing salvation, lowly and riding on a donkey, a colt, the foal of a don- key" (Zech. 9:9).

Mary was among the most exuberant of the rejoicing multitude, shouting, "Blessed is the kingdom of our father David that comes in the name of the Lord! Hosanna in the highest!" People were spreading their coats in His pathway and waving palm branches, clearly gestures reserved for a conquering king.

When the scribes and Pharisees ordered Jesus to silence the lively throng, Jesus rebuked the leaders. "If they keep quiet, the stones will cry out," He responded, as if to tell His enemies prevent the fulfillment of prophecy.

Not only were the Temple priests and ruling Pharisees indignant; they were envious that this uneducated Carpenter was receiving the praise from the people. Filled with earthly wisdom, these men saw Jesus as a serious threat to their authority, and position, and especially to national security.

As much as this interruption disturbed Mary, something else happened that troubled her even more. While descending from Olivet to Jerusalem, Jesus halted the rejoicing procession and began to gaze at the beautiful city as if in a trance. After a long silence, His face contorted with anguish and He wept over the city. There was a terrible finality in His voice when He spoke an oracle, prophesying the city's future.

"Days will come upon you when your enemies will build an embankment around you, surround you and close you in on every side, and level you, and your children within you, to the ground; and they will not leave in you one stone upon another, because you did not know the time of your visitation" (Luke 19:43, 44).

That very same day He entered the Temple and once again ex pelled the money changers, overthrowing their tables and evicting those who bought and sold in the Temple, and the sacrifice salesmen. Then, as if that were not enough, He had a verbal showdown with the Sadducees, scribes, Pharisees, and lawyers.

They wanted to trap Him in His own words, or at least embarrass and discredit Him before the people. Instead their wicked plan backfired miserably. With His supernatural wit Jesus unexpectedly turned the tables on the leaders, leaving them humiliated in front of the crowd of worshipers. Then Jesus closed the confrontation by denouncing them as hypocrites, blind fools, whitewashed tombs, and a brood of vipers!

As they stormed away, disgraced by His scathing rebukes, their burning eyes reflected the murderous vengeance fomenting in their hearts. There was no question about it. The greedy leaders would now pay any price to destroy Him.

As Jesus left the Temple He stopped to survey the beautiful edifice and said, "See! Your house is left to you desolate; for I say to you, you shall see Me no more till you say, 'Blessed is He who comes in the name of the Lord!'" (Matt. 23:38, 39). Matthew told Mary that later Jesus foretold that soon there would not be one stone of the Temple left upon another. There was no doubt—Jesus knew something ominous was about to happen.

Late that night, tossing in her bed, Mary relived the events of the week. Hours later, her restless thoughts finally surrendered to a troubled sleep.

Deep in the quiet of that mild spring night, the stillness of Martha's Bethany home was abruptly broken by the persistent pounding of a fist on the front door.

"Who is it?" Lazarus called in the dark. "What do you want?"

"It's Andrew!" came the muffled reply. Andrew was one of the most kind and thoughtful of Jesus' disciples. Mary heard her brother fumble for his robe and head for the door. From the room across the hall, Mary could see Martha blowing on a coal to light a piece of straw for the lamp. As fear rose within her, Mary leaped from her bed and slipped into her robe.

Lazarus quickly flung open the door. He abruptly drew Andrew in, then shut and barred the door behind him. "What's happened?" he asked. Even before Andrew replied, Mary knew.

"They have taken the Master," Andrew panted, struggling to catch his breath.

"Who took Him?" Martha burst into the parlor, words first.

"The priests came with the Temple guards and a great company. And—" Andrew grew pale. His voice broke with shock as he spoke. "Judas Iscariot was leading them."

"Judas?" Lazarus gasped in disbelief. Mary, standing in the shadows behind her brother, was not as surprised.

"Where did they take Him?" Martha pressed.

"I'm not sure," Andrew admitted. "We were confused and

frightened. I did see Peter, my brother, pull out his sword and swing it, but Jesus stopped him and made no effort to escape."

Lazarus led the exhausted Andrew to a couch to sit down. For a moment Andrew covered his eyes with his hand. After a long pause, he looked pleadingly into Lazarus' eyes. "When He allowed them to seize Him and tie His hands, we were all stunned! We thought He would use His power to deliver Himself as before." Andrew shame-fully lowered his head again. "When He did nothing, we all pan-icked and ran off in different directions."

Martha gasped as if unable to catch her breath. "O Lord, do not let them harm the anointed of Israel."

Unaware of the woman's prayer, Andrew continued. "I think they took Him to the house of the high priest."

Lazarus nodded his head solemnly. "They'll make short work of a trial." He heaved a heavy sigh. "Then they'll have to take Him to Pilate to secure a death decree—that is, if they don't murder Him first."

"I must find Him. I must do something." Mary hurried to her room, threw on her clothing, tied her hair in a head wrap, and re-turned to find her sister and brother ready to leave as well.

Just as the glint of the new morning began to compete with the stars, the dark forms of four frightened disciples could be faintly seen in the lingering moonlight, hurrying down the road to the holy city. Bethany was on the eastern slope of Olivet, about two miles from Jerusalem. As they crested the hill overlooking the an-cient city, Lazarus commented that it was odd to see so many lights lit in Jerusalem at such an early hour. Something unusual was in-deed happening.

"How will we find Him?" Mary asked.

Andrew was the first to respond. "First, we should go to the house of Mary, John Mark's mother. We've always left messages there in her upper room whenever we were in Jerusalem."

They hurried down the Mount of Olives, past the Garden of Gethsemane. Andrew pointed to the clearing where he had last seen Jesus, as if, perhaps, hoping he would still find Him there.

"That is where—"

From behind a grove of young cypress trees they heard a loud, pitiful moan like that of a wounded animal. The sound sent chills up Mary's spine.

It was Peter. He had returned to the garden to sob out his repentance for denying his Lord. He had thrown himself prostrate on the very spot where Jesus, a few hours earlier, had moistened the ground with His blood and His tears as He agonized in prayer. Andrew walked over, knelt beside his older brother, and tenderly placed his hand on the shoulder of the strong fisherman. Overwhelmed with grief, Peter's whole frame convulsed as he wept bitterly.

"Simon," Andrew pleaded with his sibling, "come, we are going to the upper room."

"No," Peter moaned. "I denied Him. Three times!"

Andrew attempted to console him. "We were all frightened. We all ran away."

"You don't understand. Jesus looked at me," Peter sobbed. "The last time I cursed and swore that I did not know Him, He looked right at me from the judgment hall."

Peter lifted his face toward his brother. It was covered with earth and tears. "Then, as I heard the rooster crowing, I saw a guard strike Him! Remember what He told me? He tried to warn me, but I was too proud to listen."

Peter buried his face on one arm and pounded the ground with his fist as he wept.

Lazarus assured Peter, "When we find out what's happened, we'll send someone back for you." It was obvious that this grieving disciple was in no condition to be of any help in their search. Reluctantly Andrew left his brother. He commented to Lazarus that he had not seen him cry since they were boys.

When they reached the Golden Gate, the Roman guards were too sleepy to question them, and they let them pass through without explanation. During the Passover week devoted Jewish pilgrims from all over the empire had come to Jerusalem in droves. The city guards were already dreading the onslaught that would come with approaching daylight.

This year the Passover fell on the weekly Sabbath, making it a "high Sabbath." This would bring an unusually heavy crowd, thousands of worshipers pushing to the Temple in time for the Friday afternoon sacrifice.

When Mary and the others reached John Mark's house, they found that Andrew had been right. Several of the other disciples were already there. The air was heavy with a dreadful expectation. Martha fell into John Mark's mother's arms. Mary watched as the two women wept on each other's shoulders. The room was filled with questions, everyone wanting to hear any fresh news of their captured Lord.

"We know little, aside from what Andrew told us," Martha explained. "We met Peter in the garden. He said he last saw Jesus in the high priest's judgment hall."

"What have you heard?" Mary added.

At this point 18-year-old John Mark spoke up. "I knew Jesus and the 12 would be sleeping in the garden tonight, and I wanted to hear the Master tell the Passover story again. So I came to Gethsemane. But by the time I arrived, Thomas said that Jesus seemed upset and had taken Peter, James, and John a stone's throw away so they could pray. So I talked a little with Thomas and Nathanael; then I removed my outer garments, lay down, and covered myself with the sheet and went to sleep. The next thing I heard was the sound of men shouting as a mob approached. There were soldiers with them.

"We all knew this day would come, but we expected that when they'd lay hands on Him and bind Him, the Spirit of the Lord would come upon Him and He would shake Himself free, like Samson. We thought we would follow Jesus into battle against the Romans until He claimed the throne of David." The young man looked bewildered by the strange turn of events. "But when they bound Jesus, He made no effort to resist. We were all stunned as they took Him away like a common criminal. They led Him from the garden in the direction of the city."

John Mark swallowed hard and continued. "I wrapped my sheet around me and tried to follow. Then two of the Temple guards saw me and shouted, 'Are you spying for Him?'

"They grabbed for me, but I wrestled free from their grip and fled naked, leaving my sheet in their hands."

"That's a bad omen," Thomas said as he looked down and shook his head. "That was what happened to the patriarch Joseph when he fled from Potiphar's wife. He landed in jail."

Mark ignored the negative commentary from Thomas and continued. "Before they chased me, I heard one of them say that after they held the trial they'd need to wake up Pilate to secure the death decree." John Mark searched Lazarus' eyes for understanding. "They've already decided He's guilty," he concluded. "They're determined to crucify Him before His followers hear what's happened."

The word "crucify" drew a chorus of moans from the frightened disciples. This dreaded form of execution was used on the worst of criminals. It was designed to cause the most extreme suffering for the victim.

No sooner had John Mark uttered those words than Mary knew she had to do something, anything. She flung open the door and disappeared into the night.

The hours that followed were filled with heart-wrenching frustration for Mary. By the time she reached the house of Annas, the retired high priest, Jesus had already been transferred to Caiaphas, the current priest. At Caiaphas' house a sleepy servant told her the Jewish council had condemned Him to die and were on their way to Pilate to have him ratify their death penalty. These were determined and ruthless men. They would not rest until they had achieved their goal.

On Mary's way to Pilate's judgment hall, a local merchant opening his shop told her that he had heard that Pilate had just sent Jesus to Herod's palace. "Since Jesus is from Galilee," the shopkeeper reminded her, "the prisoner is under Herod's jurisdiction."

Exhausted, Mary leaned against the wall and sobbed. Herod was the most hard-hearted and hated ruler in the Roman Empire. It was his father who had slaughtered the baby boys in Bethlehem, and the son was no less heartless. He had had John the Baptist put to death without even a semblance of a trial. She knew that Jesus would receive no mercy from this cruel man.

Regaining her breath, Mary rushed to the Roman quarter of Jerusalem, toward Herod's summer palace. Mary was so distraught that she failed to notice the morning sun bathing the housetops with the first rays of golden spring sunlight. Suddenly the terrifying morning two years earlier flashed through the woman's mind, the day she first had seen Jesus in the Temple and He had rescued her from the same evil men.

Mary realized she would not be able to do the same for Him. She understood that Jesus was now taking her punishment. "But if only I could do something for Him. If only I could just be near Him."

As soon as the grieving young woman rounded the street that entered the Roman sector, she heard the clatter of armor and the stomping of soldiers' feet. She saw in horror a throng of soldiers, led by priests, making their way up the narrow cobblestone road. In their midst, guarded on every side as if He were a dangerous convict, was Jesus. The procession moved in a hasty, determined manner. Mary had to duck quickly into a doorway to avoid being run over by this military mob.

When she finally caught a glimpse of Jesus up close, she barely recognized Him. A Roman guard drove Him up the road, occasionally whacking Him on the shoulders with the wooden handle of his whip. They had braided a crown from the vines of a brutal-looking thornbush and pressed it into His head. The back of His seamless robe was wet and shining with blood. His face was bruised and covered with a sickening mixture of blood and spittle. His beard was strangely uneven and raw, as if someone had pulled out fistfuls of hair. Yet, in spite of all this, she saw no vestige of anger marking His expression.

Her heart ached for her Master. He was the gentlest Man she'd ever known. It grieved her beyond words to see Him suffer like this. Mary felt nauseous. Tears blurred her vision.

As the procession passed, she fell in behind and asked one of the spectators, a short round man, "What happened to Him?"

The man answered, "Well, the way I heard it is that Herod wanted the Teacher to perform some miracle. The king offered to let Him go, but when He didn't respond, Herod commanded that

He be flogged. Then He was turned over to the soldiers for their entertainment."

The stranger's face hardened. "Those Roman guards were waiting for a chance to get their hands on a Jew, and they made the most of it! Now I guess Herod has sent Him back to Pilate."

Upon entering the gate of Pilate's judgment hall, Mary saw hundreds more had already gathered. People were making their way to the outer court. Some of the priests' servants were circulating through the growing mob, spreading the word, "When Pilate questions the crowd, ask for Barabbas!"

Mary strained on her toes to see what was happening, but her slight frame was jostled back and forth by the growing concourse, mostly men. She pushed her way as close to the front as possible until she was stopped by a double row of elite Roman guards who aimed their spears nervously toward the agitated mob.

Just beyond the guard, the priests and Sanhedrin leaders stood at the base of the steps. Jewish law would not permit them to venture into a Gentile's dwelling for fear of being defiled and rendered unclean. They would not want that, especially on this high and holy week of Passover.

Mary thought to herself, *What hypocrites! Here they are, about to murder an innocent Man, their Messiah, and all they can think about is not placing their foot on the doorstep of a Roman dwelling.* She thought of Jesus' words "Blind guides, who strain out a gnat and swallow a camel" (Matt. 23:24).

Mary turned to one of the few women present and asked, "What is happening to Jesus?"

Barely glancing at Mary, the woman said, "Pilate summoned Him into the hall to question Him." Mary glanced a second time at the woman and realized she recognized her. The woman had been one of the leaders in the multitude that had directed Jesus' praising procession into Jerusalem.

After several restless moments Pilate emerged from the judgment hall, looking troubled and perplexed. He had the battered form of Jesus in tow. The Lord was stationed between two pillars, with a soldier on either side. The story of Samson flashed into Mary's mind.

Pilate nodded toward Jesus. "I have examined the one you call the King of the Jews, and I find no fault in Him." The crowd grew agitated as Pilate paused before finishing his thought. "But because this is your holy week, as a gesture of good will I will do as I have done before and release one of your people." Immediately two soldiers brought out Barabbas, the most infamous Jewish villain the Romans had ever captured. Barabbas was a thief, murderer, and self-proclaimed messiah.

Pilate stood the two men before the people. The contrast could not have been more vivid. Barabbas was a cold and hardened criminal; Jesus, though marred by torture, still bore a divine innocence and majesty.

Mary could not believe her ears. Like bellowing wild beasts the crowd screeched, "Release Barabbas!" Mary noted that the servants of the priests were scattered among the throng, urging them on. Louder and louder swelled the chant, "Barabbas! Barabbas! Give us Barabbas! Release Barabbas!"

Mystified by this unexpected response, Pilate's face drained of color. "What then do you want me to do with Him whom you call the King of the Jews?" (Mark 15:12).

The chief priests answered, "We have no king but Caesar!" (John 19:15).

The crowd bellowed in unison, "Crucify Him!"

Mary screamed at the top of her lungs, "Free Jesus!" Several of the mob glared hatefully at her. But her frail lone voice was lost in the roar of the demon-possessed mob that called for His blood.

They continued chanting. "Crucify Him! Crucify Him!"

Pilate looked at the crowd with bewilderment and disgust. "Why, what evil has He done?" (Matt. 27:22).

Mary saw the woman beside her who a few days earlier had shouted "Hosanna to the Son of David! Blessed is He who comes in the name of the Lord!" now snarl, "Crucify Him! Crucify Him!"

Pilate looked clearly frustrated. "Why, what evil has He done? I have found no reason for death in Him" (verse 22). The roar of the mob became deafening.

The Roman prelate lifted his hands for silence. Reluctantly the

THE 97 STORY

agitated throng obeyed. In a tone of appeasement he said, "I will chastise Him, and let Him go." But the very mention of His release stirred the people to a tenfold frenzy. Mary heard one of the priests shout at Pilate, "If you let this Man go, you are not Caesar's friend. Whoever makes himself a king speaks against Caesar" (John 19:12).

When Pilate heard that they were accusing him of treason and saw that a riot was brewing, he took water and washed his hands before the multitude. "I am innocent of the blood of this just Person. You see to it" (Matt. 27:24).

A loud demonic cry of victory went up from the mob: "His blood be on us and on our children" (verse 25). So Pilate, wanting to gratify the crowd, released Barabbas to them and ordered that Jesus be scourged, then crucified.

Mary stood paralyzed for a few moments. She struggled with herself as others hurried to the place of execution. She longed to be near Jesus, but she was nauseated by the thought of witnessing His punishment. She'd seen crucifixions—the most horrific form of execution ever devised.

Slowly Mary turned and made her way toward the gate. It was about 9:00 in the morning, and now it seemed as though the whole city was awake and buzzing with what was about to happen. As Mary, with increasing determination, plowed her way through the growing mob up the old street, she heard the voices of the people just ahead of her grow more excited. The soldiers were shouting to clear a path as they took Jesus to the place of execution. Along with Jesus the soldiers escorted two criminals, thieves, who were to be executed at the same time.

Mary desperately pressed her way forward until she could see Jesus, but the terrible sight nearly made her faint. He was hunched over under the heavy burden of an ugly cross that had been placed on His shoulders. His hands were strapped to the crossbeam, preventing Him from shooing away the irritating insects that were now attracted to His bloody face. His legs shook with each step. Mary could see it was not so much from the weight of the cross—fresh wet blood on Jesus' back told her that Pilate's order that He be scourged again had been obeyed. The pressure of the knotty beam on His torn back must be excruciating.

Jesus stumbled and fell to His knees against the unforgiving stone pavement. An impatient Roman guard kicked Him in His side and started cursing and shouting something in Latin. Moaning from the intense pain, Jesus struggled to His feet again but managed only a couple steps before He fainted. Unable to catch His fall, He landed facedown on the stones.

Mary cringed and instinctively lunged toward Jesus to help Him. Surprised by her audacity, the same soldier that had kicked Jesus pushed her aside.

But the centurion in charge, realizing that it was impossible for Jesus to carry His own cross any farther, ordered that the cross be loosed from His shoulders. The head guard quickly scanned the faces of the spectators until he spied a strong-looking Black man who had been eyeing Jesus sympathetically. "You! Carry it!" he ordered emphatically, motioning to the ugly implement of torture.

While everyone's attention was directed to the guards hoisting the cross to the new man's shoulders, Mary rushed to Jesus' side. She took her shawl and began to wipe His bruised and bleeding face gently. She knew she had only a few seconds, and she needed water. Frantically she looked around and spied a man who had a small skin of water strapped to his belt. Without asking, Mary reached over and yanked the wooden plug from the man's water bag and squeezed the contents onto her shawl. The surprised man shouted in protest but made no effort to stop her. Mary took Jesus' head and rotated it upward, then squeezed a few drops of water from her wet cloth between His cut and swollen lips.

Jesus slowly opened His eyes. It took a few seconds for Him to focus on Mary, who was now bathing the blood from His face with the wet end of her shawl. Mary knew the moment of recognition because Jesus clearly smiled at her with His eyes. Just then the soldiers noticed what she was doing; one of them shouted and lifted his whip in a threatening gesture.

As Mary reluctantly retreated into the crowd she was thankful that in some small way she could provide a brief oasis of relief to her

Master. She was especially grateful that Jesus knew she was there. But now His nightmare must resume. With His hands freshly tied in front and a sharp Roman spear prodding Him from behind, Jesus slowly plodded on to fulfill prophecy.

As they neared the city gates one of the condemned thieves managed to free one of his hands and made a pathetic and desperate attempt to bolt for freedom—while dragging the cross still strapped to his other hand. As the guards subdued the rebel, Jesus heard a group of women at the gate weeping for Him. He turned to them and in a clear voice uttered a chilling oracle: "Daughters of Jerusalem, do not weep for Me, but weep for yourselves and for your children. For indeed the days are coming in which they will say, 'Blessed are the barren, wombs that never bore, and breasts which never nursed!' Then they will begin to say to the mountains, 'Fall on us!' and to the hills, 'Cover us!' For if they do these things in the green wood, what will be done in the dry?" (Luke 23:18-31). When Mary heard these words, she felt a shiver go down her spine.

The throng of people trying to squeeze through the Sheep Gate created a bottleneck, and Mary was forced back into the crowd. By the time she reached the hill called Calvary, the two thieves who had been condemned with Jesus were struggling desperately as a band of soldiers wrestled them into position on their crosses and pounded the spikes through their limbs. The Roman soldiers mocked at the men's terrified pleadings and agonizing cries. But as they stripped Jesus and positioned Him on the rough beams, the hardened soldiers marveled at His peaceful compliance.

Mary heard a man behind her quoting the writings of the prophets: "'He was oppressed and He was afflicted, yet He opened not His mouth; He was led as a lamb to the slaughter, and as a sheep before its shearers is silent, so He opened not His mouth' [Isa. 53:7]." She turned and recognized Nicodemus, a prominent Pharisee who had recently become openly supportive of Jesus' ministry. The great man was weeping as he cited these Messianic scriptures.

The centurion, now feeling sympathy for Jesus, had one of his guards offer Him a mixture of gall and wine to ease His pain before they spiked Him to the tree. Jesus put His mouth to the ladle, but when He realized it was old wine He refused to drink it.

Mary cringed as one of the guards swung his mallet and drove the first iron nail through the Saviour's tender, quivering flesh. Jesus arched His back and released an agonizing groan. His fingers twitched with pain, but still He bore a serene calm on His face. They repeated the gory task on His other hand, then His feet. Then she and all those gathered on the hill heard Jesus call out to the heavens, "Father, forgive them, for they do not know what they do" (Luke 23:34).

Brokenhearted and physically nauseated, Mary turned away from the scene just in time to see John on the fringe of the crowd. He and another disciple were bearing away the limp form of Jesus' mother. She had fainted.

Mary moved instinctively toward her friends. John's eyes were red from crying and fatigue. Two other women accompanied him: Mary the wife of Clopas, and Jesus' aunt. Reviving Jesus' mother, they offered to take her away, but she insisted on staying. So flanked by John and the wife of Clopas, the three of them turned to face the awful execution. No one uttered a word. With a shout the soldiers hoisted Jesus' cross into position, and with a violent thud it slid into the hole that had been prepared. Jesus let out another agonizing moan as the weight of His body abruptly shifted to the spikes.

At first it was impossible to be near Jesus. Thousands of devoted Passover pilgrims from all over the Roman Empire flooded the road leading into the city. Many stopped, gazing in shock at the crosses, and especially at the hastily scribbled sign on the middle cross. The words "This is the King of the Jews," in three languages, were nailed on a rough board above Jesus' head.

These spectators would lower their eyes, pound their breasts, and walk away. Then there were the religious leaders, who surrounded the cross like cowardly jackals waiting for their potential meal to die. They hurled taunts and curses at the dying Man. It was obvious to all watching that demons of jealousy drove these men to crucify Him, and bloodthirsty demons of cruelty possessed them now.

As the endless hours dragged by, vultures began to circle over head, and the crowds began to thin. People needed to rush home to make final preparations for the approaching Sabbath. With each opportunity Mary, along with the other faithful worshipers, moved closer to the cross until she stood a few yards from the only Man who had ever loved her with a pure love.

The hardened Roman guards stationed at the site were shocked by the cruelty demonstrated by the religious leaders against one of their own. But they eyed Mary and her friends with sympathy and allowed them to approach Jesus' cross.

Jesus' eyes were closed and His breathing labored. But as if He sensed Mary's approach, the Master opened His eyes and looked at her with an expression that said, *This is how much I love you.* As Mary gazed up through her tears into His beaten face, she instinctively reached out with one of her delicate hands and with trembling fingers briefly touched His bruised and bleeding feet.

The Study

LUKE 23:33, 34

"When they had come to the place called Calvary, there they crucified Him, and the criminals, one on the right hand and the other on the left. Then Jesus said, 'Father, forgive them, for they do not know what they do.' And they divided His garments and cast lots."

The crucifixion and sufferings of Jesus may not be a pleasant study, but it is high in spiritual nutrition. It will always inspire a deep and humble appreciation for the One who took our place as sinners. The theme of the cross is the axle upon which the gospel turns. Like the home of a morning jogger, the cross is both the starting point and the destination in the process of conversion. Paul said, "For I determined not to know any thing among you, save Jesus Christ, and him crucified" (1 Cor. 2:2, KJV).

Just as Zacchaeus climbed the tree and then saw Jesus, the vantage point of the cross will give us our best view of the Saviour (Luke 19:1-10).

THE CROSS IS THE FOCUS

When Benjamin Franklin was about to die, he asked that a picture of Christ on the cross be so placed in his bedroom that he could look, as he said, "upon the form of the Silent Sufferer."

One of my favorite authors wrote, "It will do you good . . . to frequently review the closing scenes in the life of our Redeemer. Here, beset with temptations as He was, we may all learn lessons of the utmost importance to us. It would be well to spend a thoughtful hour each day reviewing the life of Christ from the manger to Calvary.

"We should take it point by point and let the imagination vividly grasp each scene, especially the closing ones of His earthly life. By thus contemplating His teachings and sufferings, and the infinite sacrifice made by Him for the redemption of the race, we may strengthen our faith, quicken our love, and become more deeply imbued with the spirit which sustained our Saviour.

"If we would be saved at last, we must learn the lesson of penitence and faith at the foot of the cross. . . . Everything noble and generous in man will respond to the contemplation of Christ upon the cross" (*Lift Him Up,* p. 240).

There is nothing attractive about crucifixion in itself. It is an extremely ugly and revolting form of execution. But as for contemplating it, a spoonful of this medicine, bitter at first, will bring healing to our souls.

THE SUFFERING OF THE CROSS

Crucifixion was originally devised by the Persians, but the Romans developed it to extract the last ounce of suffering from the unfortunate victim. One historian wrote: "The cross upon which Jesus died consisted of a perpendicular stake with a crossbeam either at the top of the stake or shortly below the top. A block or a pin was sometimes driven into the stake to serve as a seat for the condemned person, giving partial support to his body. Sometimes a step for the feet was fixed to the stake.

"Victims of crucifixion often did not die for two or three days. Usually the victim had been severely scourged before crucifixion, which could speed the death process from loss of blood. Another factor contributing to the duration of suffering was the presence or absence of the seat and the footrest. For when a person suspended by his hands lost blood pressure quickly, the pulse rate increased. Total collapse through insufficient blood circulation to the brain and the heart followed shortly. If the victim could support himself by using the seat and footrest, the blood could be returned to some degree of circulation in the upper part of his body."

Grant Osborne graphically describes this horrible death: "To fix the victim's hands to the cross beam, either cords or nails and cords were used; sometimes the feet were also nailed. When it was desired to bring the torture to an end, the victim's legs were broken below the knees with a club. It was then no longer possible for him to ease his weight, and the loss of blood circulation accelerated his demise. Coronary insufficiency followed shortly" *(Holman Bible Dictionary).*

WHAT WAS WRITTEN ON THE CROSS?

Some have wondered why the Gospels' statements describing the sign above the head of Jesus seem to contradict one another.

1. "And they put up over His head the accusation written against Him: THIS IS JESUS THE KING OF THE JEWS" (Matt. 27:37).

2. "And the inscription of His accusation was written above: THE KING OF THE JEWS" (Mark 15:26).

3. "And an inscription also was written over Him in letters of Greek, Latin, and Hebrew: THIS IS THE KING OF THE JEWS" (Luke 23:38).

4. "Now Pilate wrote a title and put it on the cross. And the writing was: JESUS OF NAZARETH, THE KING OF THE JEWS" (John 19:19).

It is true that there are slight differences between the Gospel records. The answer as to why is found in Luke's record—it reminds us that these signs contained the statement in three different languages—"in letters of Greek, Latin, and Hebrew" (Luke 23:38).

Most of the variations in the Gospel accounts come from the text being translated from different languages. Luke and John wrote for the Gentiles; they would prefer the Greek inscription. Matthew, addressing the Jews, would use the Hebrew; Mark, writing to the Romans, would naturally give the Latin. Also, keep in mind that Pilate had the sign created, possibly by a Roman soldier who may not have been particular or capable of harmonizing the texts.

WHO WAS AT THE CROSS?

Along the same line, it might be asked why the various Gospel writers record slight differences in the list of disciples who were present at the scene of the Crucifixion: "And many women were there beholding afar off, which followed Jesus from Galilee, ministering unto him: among which was Mary Magdalene, and Mary the mother of James and Joses, and the mother of Zebedee's children" (Matt. 27:55, 56, KJV).

"There were also women looking on from afar, among whom were Mary Magdalene, Mary the mother of James the Less and of Joses, and Salome, who also followed Him and ministered to Him when He was in Galilee, and many other women who came up with Him to Jerusalem" (Mark 15:40, 41).

"But all His acquaintances, and the women who followed Him from Galilee, stood at a distance, watching these things" (Luke 23:49).

"Now there stood by the cross of Jesus His mother, and His mother's sister, Mary the wife of Clopas, and Mary Magdalene" (John 19:25).

The logical answer is that, in the seven hours that Jesus' body hung on the cross, many of His friends and disciples who believed in Him stood in small companies and viewed the nightmare from various distances. Some came and went as the hours rolled by and the Sabbath approached. Luke says they "stood at a distance." John records that they stood "by" the cross. Probably as the hours went by and the agitated crowds dissipated the loyal followers drew near.

But one thing is unmistakable—by all accounts, Mary Magdalene was there the whole time.

How does the cross work?

A young infantryman fighting in Italy during World War II jumped into a foxhole just ahead of some bullets. As he tried to deepen the hole for more protection, frantically scraping away the dirt with his hands, he unearthed a silver crucifix left by a former resident of the foxhole. A moment later another figure landed in the hole beside him. The soldier with the crucifix saw that his new companion was an Army chaplain. The foot soldier gasped, "Am I ever glad to see you! How do you make this thing work?"

Some have mistakenly taught that in Old Testament times people were saved by works but the New Testament teaches that we are saved by faith. Wrong. Everyone who is redeemed is saved by faith in the sacrifice of Jesus. All the saints from Adam to John the Baptist were saved by looking forward in faith to the cross. Everybody who is saved today is rescued by virtue of looking back in faith to the cross. Everyone is saved by faith through beholding "the Lamb of God who takes away the sin of the world" (John 1:29).

It is this simple: We cannot be saved without loving God. But how do we come to love Him? "We love Him because He first loved us" (1 John 4:19). This is why Jesus said, "And I, if I am lifted up from the earth, will draw all peoples to Myself" (John 12:32). The cross is the most concentrated point in history; it is there that we best see His love demonstrated for us. At the cross the love of God reached "critical mass"; that marvelous power draws every heart.

Peter said if we would be saved we must first repent: "Repent ye therefore, and be converted, that your sins may be blotted out" (Acts 3:19, KJV).

Well, how do we repent? The Scriptures give the answer: "The goodness of God leads you to repentance" (Rom. 2:4).

It is at the cross that we see the goodness of God best displayed. At the cross we see Satan's love for power and Jesus' power of love. The cross is the catalyst for every true conversion.

THE CROSS GIVES COURAGE

Steve Brown related the story of a British soldier in World War I who lost heart for battle and deserted. Trying to reach the coast for a boat to England that night, he ended up wandering in the pitch-black night, hopelessly lost. He came across what he thought was a signpost. The night was so dark that he climbed the post in order to read it. At the top of the pole he struck a match and found himself looking squarely into the face of Jesus Christ. He realized that, rather than climbing a signpost, he had scaled a roadside crucifix. Brown explained, "Then he remembered the One who had died for him—who had endured, who had never turned back. The next morning the soldier was back in the trenches."

"For consider Him who endured such hostility from sinners against Himself, lest you become weary and discouraged in your souls" (Heb. 12:3).

THE CROSS GIVES US POWER TO FORGIVE

Let us always keep in mind that the first words spoken from the cross were ones of forgiveness! "Then Jesus said, 'Father, forgive them, for they do not know what they do'" (Luke 23:34).

This not only assures of Jesus' desire and provision to forgive every sinner, but also answers that the cross gives us power to forgive each other. "Bearing with one another, and forgiving one another, if anyone has a complaint against another; even as Christ forgave you, so you also must do" (Col. 3:13). "For if you forgive men their trespasses, your heavenly Father will also forgive you. But if you do not forgive men their trespasses, neither will your Father forgive your trespasses" (Matt. 6:14, 15).

George Herbert said, "He who cannot forgive others breaks the bridge over which he must pass himself."

How can we find power to forgive those who have deeply wounded or hurt us? As we stand in the blazing light streaming from Calvary, every spot of sin in our own characters becomes painfully clear. It gives us a better perspective of how much Jesus has forgiven us. When we truly sense that God has freely absolved us from a virtual mountain of sin, the offenses that others have committed against us seem by comparison as molehills (Matt. 18:23-35).

Alexander C. Dejong said, "To forgive someone involves three things. First, it means to forgo the right of striking back. One rejects the urge to repay gossip with gossip and a bad turn with a worse turn. Second, it means replacing the feeling of resentment and anger with good will, a love which seeks the other's welfare, not harm. Third, it means the forgiving person takes concrete steps to restore good relations" (*Leadership,* vol. 4, No. 1).

FORGIVING AND FORGETTING

After the Civil War, Robert E. Lee visited a Kentucky woman who took him to view the remains of a grand old tree in front of her home. There she cried bitterly about how its limbs and trunk had been destroyed or damaged by Union artillery fire. She expected General Lee to condemn the North, or at least to sympathize with her loss. Lee paused, and then tenderly said, "Cut it down, my dear madam, and forget it."

Truly forgiving will mean choosing to forget. Clara Barton, the founder of the American Red Cross Society, was reminded one day of a vicious deed that someone had done to her years before. But she acted as if she had never heard of the incident. "Don't you remember it?" her friend asked.

"No," came Barton's reply. "I distinctly remember forgetting it."

But you may be thinking, *Can one really forget?* Perhaps not, but one can choose to not think about it.

Martin Luther said, "You may not be able to prevent the birds from flying over your head, but you can stop them from making a nest in your hair." Likewise, we can choose to not dwell on these forgiven issues.

IT'S HEALTHY TO HATE . . . SIN

I realize that the cross is not a pretty picture, but then neither is sin. When we consider the awfulness of the cross let us remember that it is our horrid sins that caused it. Not only does the cross teach us about the wonderful love of God, but it reminds us how disgusting sin is to God.

"But sin, that it might appear sin, was producing death in me through what is good, so that sin through the commandment might become exceedingly sinful" (Rom. 7:13).

We will never know all that Jesus endured and suffered in order for us to be saved. Not only is it true that He bore the suffering for all humanity; on the cross Jesus bore all the suffering of nature. Sin has caused great suffering to God, to our neighbor, ourselves, and even to creation. Every thorn and fading flower, every fallen sparrow and thundercloud reminds us that all of nature is suffering the consequences of sin with us. "For we know that the whole creation groans and labors with birth pangs together until now" (Rom. 8:22).

Here is another of my favorite quotes:

"The spotless Son of God hung upon the cross. His flesh lacerated with stripes; those hands so often reached out in blessing, nailed to the wooden bars; those feet so tireless on ministries of love, spiked to the tree; that royal head pierced by the crown of thorns; those quivering lips shaped to the cry of woe.

"And all that He endured—the blood drops that flowed from His head, His hands, His feet, the agony that racked His frame, and the unutterable anguish that filled His soul at the hiding of His Father's face—speaks to each child of humanity, declaring, It is for thee that the Son of God consents to bear this burden of guilt; for thee He spoils the domain of death, and opens the gates of Paradise. He who stilled the angry waves and walked the foam-capped billows, who made devils tremble and disease flee, who opened blind eyes and called forth the dead to life—offers Himself upon the cross as a sacrifice, and this from love to thee" (*The Desire of Ages,* p. 755).

THE CROSS GIVES US OUR BEARINGS

I remember reading the story of a police officer who was patrolling one night some years ago in northern England. He heard a quivering sob from a young child. Turning in the direction from whence it came, he found in the shadows a little boy sitting on a doorstep. With tears rolling down his cheeks, the child whimpered, "I'm lost, mister; please take me home."

The police officer sat down beside him and asked, "Do you know your address?"

The boy shook his head. The officer began naming the streets, trying to help the child remember where he lived. When that failed, the officer repeated the names of the shops and hotels in the area, but without success. Then he remembered that in the center of the city was a well-known church with a large white cross that towered on the steeple, high above the surrounding landscape. The cross was visible from where he and the child sat.

The officer pointed to the cross and asked, "Do you live anywhere near that?"

The boy looked up for a moment, and then his face immediately brightened. "Yes, that's it. Take me to the cross. I can find my way home from there!"

The cross still remains the starting place in the journey home for God's lost children.

> At the cross, at the cross where I first saw the light,
>   And the burden of my heart rolled away,
>   It was there by faith I received my sight,
>   And now I am happy all the day!
>
> —Isaac Watts

AT THE TOMB

The Story

A s the endless hours of the Crucifixion dragged on, the soldiers assigned to oversee the execution of Jesus and the two thieves occupied themselves by dividing the meager spoils of their conquered victims. They parceled out the lesser clothes by dividing the booty into four piles, but they recognized that Jesus' robe, though stained with blood, was seamless and of unusual quality. Mary felt her face grow hot as she saw these men tugging at the garment that she and Martha had made for their Lord. The soldiers finally decided to cast lots to determine who would claim it.

" 'They divide My garments among them, and for My clothing they cast lots.' " Mary again heard the broken voice of Nicodemus behind her, quoting from the twenty-second psalm of David.

At first, when the rulers were mocking Jesus, the two doomed thieves actually joined in reviling Him, but as the hours passed, one of them became more quiet and reflective.

One of the priests sneered as he pointed to the sign above Jesus' head, "Let the Christ, the King of Israel, descend now from the cross, that we may see and believe" (Mark 15:32). Then the thief on Jesus' left joined in, "If You are the Christ, save Yourself and us" (Luke 23:39).

But his companion on the right of Jesus called back, "Do you not even fear God, seeing you are under the same condemnation? And we indeed justly, for we receive the due reward of our deeds; but this Man has done nothing wrong" (verses 40, 41). The whole crowd grew quiet, listening to this surreal exchange among the dying trio. The second thief said to Jesus, "Lord, remember me when You come into Your kingdom" (verse 42).

Scarcely had the words escaped his lips when Jesus responded. "Assuredly, I say to you today, you will be with Me in Paradise" (verse 43). Mary noticed a heavenly peace settle over the face of the perishing man.

Nearly six hours had passed from the time the soldiers had pounded the spikes into Jesus' hands and feet and hoisted the cross into position. Confident that His doom was sealed, and having vented their verbal revenge until they were hoarse, a few of the priests left for their homes, under the pretense of needing to make final preparations for the Sabbath. In reality many of them were unnerved by the eerie darkness that had settled over the land, as though some divine judgment was looming.

Several of the disciples had been watching from a distance, pounding their chests and grieving over this devastating turn of events. John was still standing beside Jesus' mother, and now his own mother joined them. Knowing that Jesus' time was running out, together they cautiously drew near to the cross.

The Saviour struggled to look down from the cross at His faithful friends. Weakly He tried to blink away the dried blood and hungry flying insects from His eyes so that He might focus. Looking first at His mother and then nodding toward John by her side, He said, "Woman, behold your son!" Then He turned his eyes to John and said, "Behold your mother!" As He said this He clearly nodded toward Mary of Nazareth, not John's natural mother. The wife of Zebedee was deeply moved by the thoughtfulness of Jesus for His own mother during His dying hours.

John also realized that Jesus was committing the care of His dearest earthly tie to His closest friend. John moved closer to Mary and placed a sympathetic arm around her shoulders, indicating that he understood and accepted this sacred, living legacy. And from that hour on, John and his mother took Mary into their own home and treated her as family.

Jesus' breathing grew more shallow. As He hung limp from the spikes in His hands, it was nearly impossible to speak above a whisper. He tried to push Himself up, but this transferred more weight to the nails in His feet. This made Him tremble with new waves of pain. Hoarsely He choked out a dire plea, "I thirst!" (John 19:28). Suddenly Jesus took in a chestful of air and cried with a loud voice, in His native Aramaic, saying, *"Eloi, Eloi, lama sabachthani!"*—My God, My God, why have You forsaken Me?" (Mark 15:34).

Some of the Romans who stood close by misunderstood this declaration. Knowing the Jews were waiting for the return of Elijah, they said, "This Man is calling for Elijah!" One of the men took a sponge, filled it with sour wine vinegar, put it on a reed, and offered it to Him to drink.

Hoping this was water, Jesus craned His neck to the sponge to soothe His swollen, parched lips. Upon tasting the bitter potion, He turned away His head, even though His dry throat cried out for any moisture. It was imperative that He keep His mind clear, for the eternal fate of the lost human race was at stake.

The presence of Satan himself could be felt in the vicinity. He was working desperately, with all his cunning and power, to entice the Son of God to sin just once. He knew that then all humanity would be hopelessly lost.

Suddenly Jesus cried out again, with trumpetlike resonance, "Father, into Your hands, I commit my spirit!" (Luke 23:46). Then with a clear tone of triumph He announced, "It is finished!" (John 19:30).

With those words the last mortal breath passed from the Saviour's lungs. His bloody head dropped till His chin rested limp on His chest. There was a moment of deafening silence, then black, angry clouds began to swirl and clash overhead, as though nature itself was mourning and protesting the death of the Creator. The very earth began to shiver; soon the quivering grew into a full-blown earthquake.

Just as the panic-stricken people began to yelp and pray, the quaking stopped.

When the centurion in charge of the execution beheld this rapid and supernatural sequence of events, he was compelled by the Spirit of God to articulate what all were thinking: "Truly this Man was the Son of God!" (Mark 15:39).

After Jesus had died and the ground had ceased trembling, a dreadful silence hung in the air. The remaining leaders who had been foremost in mocking Christ now wore pale, twisted, stupefied expressions. Their discomfiture was compounded when next a terror-stricken messenger from the Temple came running and shouting that all of Jerusalem was in a state of panic and confusion.

"Just before the priest offered the Passover sacrifice," the messenger said, "the holy veil inside the Temple was torn in two, exposing the Holiest Place. The shocked priest dropped his knife, while the lamb wiggled free from his cords and disappeared into the horrified crowd."

The Pharisees looked gravely at one another. This was a very bad omen. As if wanting to conceal the evidence of their crime, the leaders hastened to the city and to Pilate's palace. They asked that Jesus' body and the others be removed from the crosses so as not to cast a morbid shadow on the holy proceedings of the Sabbath.

Pilate, knowing that death from crucifixion could take several days, was amazed to learn that Jesus had died so soon. He gave orders that the legs of the two thieves be broken to accelerate their demise.

Mary heard that among the Pharisees who approached Pilate was Joseph, a good and just man from Arimathea. Joseph was a noble member of the Sanhedrin council, who was longing for the kingdom of God. He had not consented to the decision of the other rulers to execute Jesus. When the other leaders left Pilate's presence, Joseph lingered behind and asked the governor if he could be granted the body of Jesus to give Him a decent burial.

Pilate was surprised to see that one of the paranoid group seemed to respect the Galilean. He nodded to Joseph's request and said, "Once the soldiers establish that He is indeed dead, you can take charge of the body." As a scribe was writing up a permit reflecting Pilate's orders, the governor commented to Joseph, "My wife had a troubling dream about this Man last night. You know, there was something different about Him."

"Yes, I know," Joseph responded.

By the time Joseph returned to Golgotha, the soldiers had just finished breaking the legs of the two thieves on either side of Jesus. They were both only semiconscious from the unbearable pain and their inability to raise themselves and breathe. Their bodies hung grotesquely from their hands and they sucked in air in short, labored gasps.

The remaining crowd of scoffers, satisfied that their task was complete, began to dissipate, taking with them a terrible sense of foreboding that something ominous had happened on the hill of Calvary that day.

But Mary, with John and the mother of Jesus, along with some of the other disciples and loyal friends, refused to abandon their watch. Mary saw Joseph present a paper to the centurion wherein Pilate had granted him custody of Jesus' body. The centurion, in turn, ordered his men to lower the cross so the disciples could remove the remains of their Leader. But before this was done, one of the hardened soldiers, wanting to confirm that Jesus was indeed dead—and perhaps to vent a final insult on the Jewish nation—jabbed his spear into the side of Jesus' body. Immediately two distinct streams poured from the wound—one of blood, the other clear, like water. The surprised guards stood back and waited until the strange flow stopped, then commenced lowering the tree.

"A broken heart." For the first time that day, Mary heard Matthew speak. "He died from a broken heart," Matthew said, pointing to the puddle of water and blood mingling at the foot of the cross. "That is what causes the blood and water to separate."

Mary was wondering how this former publican would know such things, but she still believed he was right.

As tenderly as possible, the disciples removed the ugly nails from the hands and feet of their fallen Leader. Joseph took charge of the operation, telling the small assembly that he believed that Jesus was a great prophet of God. He explained that if they would allow him, he would like to donate his own tomb, which was located in a nearby garden. Having no contingency plan for this tragedy, they all humbly accepted Joseph's generous offer.

Just then Nicodemus appeared with two servants. After Jesus had died, he had gone to the city and purchased an expensive mixture of myrrh and aloes, along with some linen to wrap Jesus' body. Joseph provided a stretcher to transport His remains. As they began their solemn march to the tomb, Mary saw Nicodemus walk back to the cross and take the sign declaring "Jesus, the King of the Jews." He carefully rolled the parchment and placed it in his robe.

When the little group reached the tomb they were pleased to see it was surrounded by a beautiful garden area. Joseph instructed them to spread a sheet on the ground and straighten Jesus' battered body in preparation for cleaning and wrapping before placing it in the tomb. Mary placed her hand on the arm of Jesus' mother and asked with pleading eyes if she could wrap His feet. His mother nodded and said, "I remember the first time I wrapped Him in strips of cloth and laid Him in a stone trough for feeding animals. It was not far from here." Then she added, "He was such a good little baby." At that she broke into a fresh outburst of tears.

Only a few remaining streaks of sunlight gilded the western clouds as Joseph and the women finished wrapping the still form of God's Son and placed Him on a stone ledge inside the tomb. They could hear the trumpet echo from the walls of Jerusalem signaling the late hour. "The sun will soon be down," Joseph of Arimathea called into the opening of the grave where the women were lingering. He gently cautioned them that the holy Sabbath was fast approaching.

Mary, Clopas' wife, looked around and suddenly realized how dark it had become in the tomb. "The Master would not be pleased if we desecrate the sacred hours of His Sabbath, even with our labor of love," she said.

Mary knelt, silently weeping, her hand resting on Jesus' wrapped feet. His body now looked like a butterfly cocoon. Mary thought, *Oh, if only He could throw aside this cloth and spread His wings!*

Mary felt a hand on her shoulder. It was Martha. Ever since Mary had left the upper room that morning, Martha had worried about her younger sister. She had managed to track her to the tomb, knowing if she could find Jesus she would find Mary close by. "Let's go home now, Mary," she urged. But Mary didn't move. Her moist eyes focused on a drop of blood that had managed to seep through the new white linen. Only a few weeks earlier the two sisters had performed this same task for their brother Lazarus, but there was no blood then. Now Lazarus was alive and Jesus was dead.

Could this really have happened? Martha knew it would be especially difficult for her younger sister to leave Jesus' side. "We can still prepare spices and oil before the Sabbath, and complete our task when the sacred hours are past," she said.

A dazed Mary slowly stepped from the tomb, almost walking backwards in an effort to keep her eyes on Jesus' body. She felt as though her heart would be buried with the Master.

John and several of the other apostles stood outside the garden. The heavy silence was broken as Philip pounded his fist on his breast. "How could they do it? He never hurt anyone!"

With tears Thomas added, "We should never have left Him! We forsook Him."

At a signal from Joseph, several strong men with poles and levers rolled the massive stone into position.

Mary touched Joseph's arm. "Kind sir, we are not finished preparing His body!"

"I know, madam," Joseph responded with his head bowed, "but we can't leave the tomb open. The animals will come . . ."

Meanwhile, Joseph's servants were having difficulty budging the huge stone. They looked toward the disciples. "Master, could these Galileans help us?" they asked.

Though numb with grief, the disciples shuffled over to the stone and added their strength to the grim task. Only with all straining together did they finally succeed in rolling the enormous stone into position.

Seeing the tomb sealed with the large stone brought a terrible and final reality to the events of the day. Mary burst into a new wave of tears and sobbing, which soon brought a chain reaction of grieving from the whole small assembly of disciples.

As one by one they recovered their composure, they reluctantly walked away from the tomb. Between sobs Mary asked her sister,

"How will we get back inside to finish preparing His body?"

Before Martha could answer, Jesus' mother said, "God will provide a way."

The Study

LUKE 23:50-56

"Now behold, there was a man named Joseph, a council member, a good and just man. He had not consented to their counsel and deed. He was from Arimathea, a city of the Jews, who himself was also waiting for the kingdom of God. This man went to Pilate and asked for the body of Jesus. Then he took it down, wrapped it in linen, and laid it in a tomb that was hewn out of the rock, where no one had ever lain before. That day was the Preparation, and the Sabbath drew near. And the women who had come with Him from Galilee followed after, and they observed the tomb and how His body was laid. Then they returned and prepared spices and fragrant oils. And they rested on the Sabbath according to the commandment."

MARK 15:43-46, KJV

"Joseph of Arimathaea, an honourable counsellor, which also waited for the kingdom of God, came, and went in boldly unto Pilate, and craved the body of Jesus. And Pilate marvelled if he were already dead: and calling unto him the centurion, he asked him whether he had been any while dead. And when he [Pilate] knew it of the centurion, he gave the body to Joseph. And he [Joseph] bought fine linen, and took him down, and wrapped him in the linen, and laid him in a sepulchre which was hewn out of a rock, and rolled a stone unto the door of the sepulchre."

JOHN 19:38-42

"After this, Joseph of Arimathea, being a disciple of Jesus, but secretly, for fear of the Jews, asked Pilate that he might take away the body of Jesus; and Pilate gave him permission. So he came and took the body of Jesus. And Nicodemus, who at first came to Jesus by night, also came, bringing a mixture of myrrh and aloes, about a hundred pounds. Then they took the body of Jesus, and bound it in strips of linen with the spices, as the custom of the Jews is to bury. Now in the place where He was crucified there was a garden, and in the garden a new tomb in which no one had yet been laid. So there they laid Jesus, because of the Jews' Preparation Day, for the tomb was nearby."

RESTING IN THE TOMB

In his immortal book *Pilgrim's Progress* John Bunyan wrote, "I saw in my dream that just as Christian came up to the cross, his burden loosed from his shoulders and fell from his back and began to tumble till it came to the mouth of the sepulcher, where it fell in and I saw it no more. Then was Christian glad and lightsome and said with a merry heart, 'He has given me rest by his sorrow, and life by his death.'"

It's amazing how the religious leaders at Jesus' crucifixion could be so obsessed with the letter of the law, not wanting the bodies left on the crosses during the Sabbath, and entirely missing the spirit of the law. Jesus was the very essence of the Sabbath-day rest.

In the great invitation Jesus beckons, "Come to Me, all you who labor and are heavy laden, and I will give you rest" (Matt. 11:28).

It was no coincidence that Jesus died just before the Sabbath began. He had completed His work of redemption when He declared, "It is finished!" Then through the Sabbath He rested in the tomb from His work of saving man. He rose Sunday morning to continue His work as our high priest, pleading His own blood and merits before the Father. On the first Sabbath day, in Eden, the Lord rested from His work of creation. Now Jesus was resting from His work of re-creation.

It is interesting to note that Jesus spent seven hours on the cross. He suffered six hours, from what we would call 9:00 a.m. till 3:00 p.m. After He died, He rested quietly on the cross for about an hour while Joseph obtained permission to remove and bury His body (Mark 15:25, 34).

Jesus spent seven hours on the cross: six hours suffering and one resting.

Some have suggested that by Jesus' death and resurrection He abolished or changed the Sabbath day. Nothing could be further from the truth. In fact, Jesus' disciples were so conscious of His reverence for this holy day that they would not even venture to finish embalming His body for fear of desecrating the Sabbath with their labor of love.

They returned home and prepared spices and fragrant oils. Then they rested on the Sabbath according to the commandment (Luke 23:56).

NAILED TO THE CROSS

Though the Ten Commandments were not changed or abrogated by the death of Jesus, it is true that certain ceremonial laws were canceled or fulfilled by the death of Christ. Paul writes: "And you, being dead in your sins and the uncircumcision of your flesh, hath he quickened together with him, having forgiven you all trespasses; blotting out the handwriting of ordinances that was against us, which was contrary to us, and took it out of the way, nailing it to his cross; and having spoiled principalities and powers, he made a shew of them openly, triumphing over them in it. Let no man therefore judge you in meat, or in drink, or in respect of an holyday, or of the new moon, or of the sabbath days: which are a shadow of things to come; but the body is of Christ" (Col. 2:13-17, KJV).

So what laws were nailed to the cross of Jesus? This is a very important question. The answer is given in the text just quoted—"the handwriting of ordinances that was against us." The Ten Commandments were written by the finger of God (Ex. 31:18), but the ceremonial laws were written by the hand of Moses: "Only if they are careful to do all that I have commanded them, according to the whole law and the statutes and the ordinances by the hand of Moses" (2 Chron. 33:8).

It was the ceremonial laws such as circumcision, which is specifically mentioned in Colossians 2:13, and annual Jewish sabbath days such as Passover that were nailed to the cross. The seventh-day Sabbath was part of the Decalogue and dates back to Eden, before sin, as part of God's perfect eternal plan (Gen. 2:2, 3). The seventh-day Sabbath is of an enduring nature and will still be observed by the redeemed even in the new earth (Isa. 56:6; 66:23). The Ten Commandments were written on stone, and it is impossible to nail stone to wood.

HIS LAST WILL

In the final hours of Jesus' life, as He hung on the cross He uttered His last will and testament regarding His most treasured assets. He bequeathed His clothes to the world, His forgiveness to His enemies, His mother to the disciple John, and His spirit to His Father.

When Jesus was born, His mother had gently wrapped Him in strips of cloth and laid Him in a manger. Now she had to do it again and lay Him in a tomb (John 19:40-42). His friends took the body of Jesus and bound it in strips of linen with the spices, as was the custom of the Jews in burial.

"When Joseph had taken the body, he wrapped it in a clean linen cloth, and laid it in his new tomb which he had hewn out of the rock; and he rolled a large stone against the door of the tomb, and departed. And Mary Magdalene was there, and the other Mary, sitting opposite the tomb" (Matt. 27:59-61).

DEAD TO SIN

When the pirate captains of old buried their treasure chests, to preserve the secret of the treasure's location often they would kill the sailor who helped them dig the hole, saying, "Dead men tell no tales." It's true that dead people do not talk, lie, or sin. It may sound like a paradox, but Christians cannot fully live until they first spiritually die.

"Then Jesus said to His disciples, 'If anyone desires to come after Me, let him deny himself, and take up his cross, and follow Me. For whoever desires to save his life will lose it, but whoever loses his life for My sake will find it'" (Matt. 16:24, 25).

Dead bodies are never offended at a funeral. They never sit up and complain about what is said during the eulogy, or worry that they are not being buried in their favorite clothes.

Most often, the reason we sin, lose our temper, or pout is that the old carnal, selfish nature is not dead and buried with Jesus. This is why Paul said, "For he who has died has been freed from sin" (Rom. 6:7), and "I die daily" (1 Cor. 15:31).

In Romans 6:11 we read, "Likewise reckon ye also yourselves to be dead indeed unto sin, but alive unto God through Jesus Christ our Lord" (KJV). To claim this promise, we must become dead to the sinful habits that formerly enslaved us. Just as a corpse cannot be tempted because it can't respond to temptation, so also Christians will be unresponsive to temptation if they are dead to sin. Say to yourself: "I can no more respond to that sinful temptation than a dead person could. I consider myself to be dead to that sinful thing."

It seems that our minds are geared to remember things in "threes," so when you are tempted by Satan on any point, remember this "one-two-three" plan and say it out loud:

1. "No! I choose to not do this sin anymore."
2. "Thank You, God, for the victory."
3. "I'm dead to this sin."

When Mary left the tomb she was dead to sin.

MOST FAMOUS VERSE

Probably one of the most well-known, beloved, and memorized verses in the Bible is John 3:16. But I would venture to guess that if you were to ask average Christians what the two verses that precede John 3:16 are, not one in 50 could quote them. Most people forget that that immortal verse is the continuation of a thought found in the preceding two verses. Here they are together:

"And as Moses lifted up the serpent in the wilderness, even so must the Son of man be lifted up: that whosoever believeth in him should not perish, but have eternal life. For God so loved the world, that he gave his only begotten Son, that whosoever believeth in him should not perish, but have everlasting life" (John 3:14-16, KJV).

In these three verses you have in microcosm the entire great controversy, the cosmic conflict between the serpent and the Lord. Let's look at the original story once again.

"And the people spoke against God and against Moses: 'Why have you brought us up out of Egypt to die in the wilderness? For there is no food and no water, and our soul loathes this worthless bread.' So the Lord sent fiery serpents among the people, and they bit the people; and many of the people of Israel died" (Num. 21:5, 6).

Remember that sin entered the world when the serpent, the devil, succeeded in tempting our first parents to doubt God's word. In this story in Numbers, after the Israelites rejected God's bread (bread is a symbol for Jesus and the Bible), the serpents bit them. It is the Word of God that keeps us from sin (Ps. 119:11). Let's read on in Numbers:

"Therefore the people came to Moses, and said, 'We have sinned, for we have spoken against the Lord and against you; pray to the Lord that He take away the serpents from us.' So Moses prayed for the people. Then the Lord said to Moses, 'Make a fiery serpent, and set it on a pole; and it shall be that everyone who is bitten, when he looks at it, shall live.' So Moses made a bronze serpent, and put it on a pole; and so it was, if a serpent had bitten anyone, when he looked at the bronze serpent, he lived" (Num. 21:7-9).

A SNAKE ON A STICK

For this nation of shepherds, the serpent lifted on a pole had a strong symbolism that they all understood well. Snakes are a deadly menace to sheep. A dog might get bitten by a rattlesnake and survive without any special treatment, but sheep are much more at risk. This is one of the reasons shepherds carry rods with them.

When I lived in the desert mountains, I had a snake stick that served a couple purposes. If I found a venomous intruder in my cave I would club it on the head to "bruise his head." But a snake, though mortally wounded, might continue to thrash and writhe for hours. So rather than risk grabbing it with my hand, I would lift it up with the rod to move it far away from my premises. A snake on a stick is a vivid symbol of a defeated serpent. But even beyond this, there is a much richer prophetic significance to this symbol. In the book *Patriarchs and Prophets,* Ellen G. White writes:

"All who have ever lived upon the earth have felt the deadly sting of 'that old serpent, called the devil, and Satan' (Rev. 12:9). The fatal effects of sin can be removed only by the provision that God has made. The Israelites saved their lives by looking upon the uplifted serpent. That look implied faith. They lived because they believed God's word, and trusted in the means provided for their recovery. So the sinner may look to Christ, and live. He receives pardon through faith in the atoning sacrifice. Unlike the inert and lifeless symbol, Christ has power and virtue in Himself to heal the repenting sinner" (p. 431).

"The people well knew that in itself the serpent had no power to help them. It was a symbol of Christ. As the image made in the likeness of the destroying serpents was lifted up for their healing, so One made 'in the likeness of sinful flesh' was to be their Redeemer (Rom. 8:3)" (*The Desire of Ages,* pp. 174, 175).

Jesus said: "And I, if I am lifted up from the earth, will draw all peoples to Myself" (John 12:32). It is by looking to Jesus on the cross that we are drawn by His love for us. By gazing in faith at our Redeemer's sacrifice, we are saved from the sting of the serpent.

TWO THIEVES, TWO CHOICES

The thief who was redeemed in the eleventh hour is an example of someone being saved by beholding Jesus lifted up. The two thieves who were crucified with Jesus represent the two great classes of people who have ever lived or ever will live—the saved and the lost; the righteous and the wicked. Notice the ways that these two doomed men represent all humanity:

1. Both were guilty of rebellion, murder, and stealing. We, too, have sinned and come short of the glory of God. We have all rebelled against our Maker's will, committed murder in our hearts, and robbed God of the time, means, and talents He has lent to us (Rom. 3:23).

2. They could do nothing to save themselves. Picture them hanging there naked, helpless, hands and feet spiked to a cross. I cannot think of a more vivid picture of individuals unable to rescue themselves. Yet we are just as helpless to save ourselves by our good works as were those two thieves to effect an escape from the cross.

3. The two of them had an equal opportunity to be saved. Though helpless to save themselves, they were in the immediate presence of the greatest dynamo of love and power in the whole cosmos. But they must reach their souls out in faith and ask Him. We, too, are ever in the presence of the Saviour; He is only a prayer away (Ps. 139:7). But multitudes will be lost needlessly while hoping and desiring to be saved, because they do not perform the simple act of asking (John 16:24).

Even though He was suffering the most intense agony imaginable,

Jesus never failed to hear a sincere cry for help. The devil could nail His loving hands to a tree, but he could not prevent the Saviour from saving.

In the story of the thief on the cross we have the plan of salvation in microcosm. In those four verses (Luke 23:40-43) we can see the believing thief pass through all the steps of salvation and experience all the elements necessary for conversion:

1. He saw Jesus "lifted up." "And I, if I be lifted up from the earth, will draw all men unto me" (John 12:32, KJV).

2. He believed in Christ as the spotless Lamb. "This Man has done nothing wrong" (Luke 23:41).

3. He repented and confessed his guilt. "And we indeed justly, for we receive the due reward of our deeds" (verse 41).

4. He testified publicly, in spite of the ridicule, that Jesus was his Lord and King. "Lord, . . . Your kingdom" (verse 42).

5. He asked for forgiveness. "Lord, remember me" (verse 42).

6. He suffered with Jesus.

7. He died with Christ, and in Christ. "I have been crucified with Christ; it is no longer I who live, but Christ lives in me" (Gal. 2:20).

NEW AND OLD WINE

In the Bible wine is a symbol of the blood of the covenant. Remember, after Jesus held up the cup of wine at the Last Supper He said, "For this is my blood of the new testament, which is shed for many for the remission of sins. But I say unto you, I will not drink henceforth of this fruit of the vine, until that day when I drink it new with you in my Father's kingdom" (Matt. 26:28, 29, KJV).

Keep in mind that this was new wine, unfermented grape juice. In Scripture, fermented wine represents sin and a corrupted gospel, with the intoxicating doctrines of devils. Speaking of the apostate church, the book of Revelation declares, "'I will show you the judgment of the great harlot . . . , with whom the kings of the earth committed fornication, and the inhabitants of the earth were made drunk with the wine of her fornication. . . . I saw the woman, drunk with the blood of the saints and with the blood of the martyrs of Jesus" (17:1-6).

In Jesus' first miracle He turned water into new wine at a wedding feast in Cana. He began His ministry by giving fresh wine in the context of a wedding (John 2:1-11).

Jesus is the groom, and the church is the bride. "Husbands, love your wives, just as Christ also loved the church" (Eph. 5:25).

In His last moments on the cross He tasted the sour wine offered by His tormentors. "After this, Jesus, knowing that all things were now accomplished, that the Scripture might be fulfilled, said, 'I thirst!' Now a vessel full of sour wine was sitting there; and they filled a sponge with sour wine, put it on hyssop, and put it to His mouth. So when Jesus had received the sour wine, He said, 'It is finished!' And bowing His head, He gave up His spirit" (John 19:28-30).

Jesus did not get drunk before He died. Matthew's Gospel makes it clear that He simply "tasted" the wine. When He recognized its potency He would not drink it, but He did taste it. "They gave Him sour wine mingled with gall to drink. But when He had tasted it, He would not drink" (Matt. 27:34). Back at the wedding party, the site of Jesus' first miracle, when the ruler of the feast tasted the water that was made into wine, he asked the host why he had saved the best for last (John 2:9, 10).

Up until the death of Jesus, the only blood offered for the sins of humanity was the blood of animals. This was a symbol of the blood of Jesus. But an animal's blood could never wash away our sins. Like the host at the wedding feast, God the Father saved the best blood for last when He sent Jesus.

It is interesting to note that the first miracle Jesus performed was to give a human family miraculous new wine, a symbol of His blood that would cleanse us and make us worthy to partake of the marriage supper of the Lamb (Rev. 19:9). The last thing He did before He uttered "It is finished" was to taste the sour wine offered by sinful men. The Saviour traded blood with us and tasted sin and death for every person.

WATER, BLOOD, AND NEW LIFE

On Thursday night after Jesus initiated the new covenant He led the disciples across the Kidron Valley. The Jewish historian Josephus tells us that during the Passover week so many animals were sacrificed in the Temple that the Kidron ran red with blood. This means that Jesus would have had to cross over the blood to reach the Garden of Gethsemane—where He sweat His own blood. The blood of lambs met its antitype that night in the blood of God's Lamb (Luke 22:44).

Just as a baby is born through blood and water, the church was born from the streams of blood and water that sprang from the broken heart of Jesus. Just as God put Adam to sleep and from his side brought out Adam's wife, so the Father put Jesus to sleep and a spear brought from His side a flow of blood and water, and His bride, the church, was born.

From A.D. 1347 to 1351 the Black Death ravaged Europe, killing between one quarter and one third of the population, about 25 million people. The British Isles alone lost about 800,000; in all the world as many as 75 million perished! This terrible plague, a vicious form of bubonic plague that covered the body with a black rash, was the worst in history.

It was not known at the time that the disease was transmitted to humans by fleas from rats. Today we know that one cure for the Black Death is to receive a blood transfusion from someone of the same blood type who's been exposed to the plague but has not succumbed.

In like manner, the only cure for the disease of sin is to receive a transfusion from Jesus, the only Man to live in this sinful world who did not become infected. Jesus came to give the human race a blood transfusion to save us from the disease of sin. He thirsted that we might have our parched souls quenched with living water.

LOVE WILL SUFFER TO SAVE

As legend has it, during the time of Oliver Cromwell a young soldier in England fell asleep at his guard post. The soldier was tried in military court and sentenced to death. He was to be shot at the "ringing of the curfew bell." Hearing about this, his fiancée climbed up into the bell tower several hours before curfew time and tied herself to the bell's huge clapper. When at curfew time the attendant yanked on the bell's rope and only muffled sounds came from the tower, Cromwell demanded to know why the bell was not ringing. His soldiers went to investigate and returned with the young woman. She was badly cut, bruised, and bleeding from being knocked back and forth against the great bell. Cromwell was so moved with her willingness to suffer in behalf of someone she loved that he released the soldier, saying, "Curfew shall not ring tonight."

On that rocky hill outside Jerusalem long ago, three prisoners were executed, but there was a vast difference between them. One died *to* sin, one died *in* sin, and One died *for* sin. Christ died for our sins; now we must choose if we will die in our sins or, by faith in Jesus, die to our sins.

CHAPTER
THE RESURRECTION
SEVEN

The Story

M artha gently urged Jesus' mother to come to her home for the Sabbath. "I know you have family in Bethlehem, Mary, but it is twice as far to travel. And when the Sabbath is past we can return together to embalm His body."

Noticing John standing at her side—they'd all heard the dying Jesus commit the care of His mother to the young apostle— Martha added, "Of course, John, you are always welcome." She also included Mary the wife of Clopas in her invitation. "With Lazarus staying in Jerusalem with the other disciples, we have plenty of room."

Clopas' wife thanked Martha but declined. "My husband is afraid that Caiaphas will try to have all of Jesus' followers arrested. He thinks it would be safer if I went to Emmaus. But I will return to help you at the tomb come first day."

At twilight the small company of mourners entered the village of Bethany and found the little town had not escaped the effects of the earthquake. They noted that an old wall by the side of the road had been reduced to rubble, and saw some listing barns. When they reached Martha's home they were thankful there was no serious damage there. The women and John waited outside while Martha went inside to light a lamp.

The younger Mary began weeping. Then the mother of Jesus spoke, as if in a dream: "The spring air tonight is so clear and mild. How different it is from the sky earlier today! I vividly remember it was a night like this more than 34 years ago when the angel of the Lord appeared and told me I would be His mother."

Mary Magdalene's sobbing subsided, and she studied the face of this remarkable woman reflected in the Passover moonlight.

The mother of Jesus continued, "Now I know what the prophet Simeon meant. When Jesus was an infant, Simeon prophesied that a sword would pierce through my own soul. I know now that this is the day of which he spoke."

Martha returned to the door, and they all filed into her home. The flickering light from the clay lamp danced on the walls and ceiling as the small group sat for several hours in shocked silence, staring at the small flame. Mary was still grateful that her sister, Martha, had invited them here. It warmed her heart, being close to the ones who loved Him most. She sat staring, numb and mesmerized by the little light. She was startled to reality when she saw a moth fly into the flame, then drop wounded and fluttering by the lamp.

In the devastating distractions of the day, Martha had neglected to add oil to the lamp, so as they watched, the little flame, starved of fuel, slowly faded. One by one the mourners retired to various corners of the dwelling to rest until dawn. From time to time throughout the night, someone would release an involuntary moan or a sob as the awful reality of the day's events broke afresh.

Mary lay on her usual cot by the kitchen. A few days earlier Lazarus had pulled back the summer tiles from the roof over the cooking area. This made it possible for her to look up and see the stars. They were so clear and beautiful. Why was there so much suffering and death in the world? She prayed in her heart, *Father, I don't understand why all this has happened, but I believe You are good, because Jesus said He was just like You. I will still trust You. But please, help me understand. How can I live without Him?* Somehow, Mary felt a familiar peace after communing with the Father, and she finally drifted off to sleep, thoroughly exhausted.

On the following morning they dressed for Sabbath. Wanting to avoid the crowds, they chose to go to the small synagogue in Bethany. Only a few people were there—some children under 12 who were too young to attend the feast, and a few of the older folks not strong enough to make the journey to Jerusalem. Everyone else was in the city for the Passover.

The hours of the Sabbath that had always been so rich and blessed with Jesus present now seemed hollow without Him. As the old rabbi stood to read from the book of the prophets, he chose to read from the scroll of Isaiah, beginning where he had left off the previous week: " 'Surely He has borne our griefs and carried our sorrows; yet we esteemed Him stricken, smitten by God, and afflicted. But He was wounded for our transgressions, He was bruised for our iniquities; the chastisement for our peace was upon Him, and by His stripes we are healed.

" 'All we like sheep have gone astray; we have turned, every one, to his own way; and the Lord has laid on Him the iniquity of us all.

" 'He was oppressed and He was afflicted, yet He opened not His mouth; He was led as a lamb to the slaughter, and as a sheep before its shearers is silent, so He opened not His mouth.

" 'He was taken from prison and from judgment, and who will declare His generation? For He was cut off from the land of the living; for the transgressions of My people He was stricken. And they made His grave with the wicked—but with the rich at His death, because He had done no violence, nor was any deceit in His mouth.

" 'Yet it pleased the Lord to bruise Him; He has put Him to grief. When You make His soul an offering for sin, He shall see His seed, He shall prolong His days, and the pleasure of the Lord shall prosper in His hand. He shall see the travail of His soul, and be satisfied. By His knowledge My righteous Servant shall justify many, for He shall bear their iniquities' " (Isa. 53:4-11).

Long before the rabbi finished reading, the grieving disciples began to look at one another in astonishment. By their glances they knew they were thinking the same thing. *Could this Messianic prophecy be speaking of Jesus?* They remembered when, three years earlier, John the Baptist declared that Jesus was "the Lamb of God who takes away the sin of the world!"

Back at the house, Martha served a simple meal, but none could bring themselves to eat. As they gathered about the table, John said, "Now I understand what the Master meant when He said, 'Can the friends of the bridegroom mourn as long as the bridegroom is with them? But the days will come when the bridegroom will be taken away from them, and then they will fast'" (Matt. 9:15).

Later that Sabbath afternoon Lazarus arrived from the city with Thomas. The small band of women plied them with questions.

These two disciples were an interesting pair. Lazarus was the eternal optimist, while Thomas often focused on negative possibilities.

"The Passover services in the Temple today were in total disarray," Thomas said. "Evidently, when the Master gave up the spirit yesterday, the thick veil in the Temple was torn from top to bottom, exposing the Holy of Holiest!"

Lazarus added, "Priests in the Temple said it looked as though the hand of an angel had torn the curtain in two."

"Yes, but the high priest claims it was caused from the earthquake yesterday." Thomas' cynicism could be heard in his tone.

Lazarus continued, "We also heard today that the religious leaders approached Pilate to secure a centurion and his soldiers to guard the tomb. They claim we might be planning to steal the Lord's body."

"You mean they went to Pilate on the holy Sabbath?" innocent John chimed in. "What hypocrites! When they had Pilate try Jesus, they would not even go into the judgment hall while the people were watching, under pretense of not wanting to defile themselves."

A frown deepened on Martha's face. "That's not the issue, John. We already knew that these men are corrupt. The question is How will we finish anointing His body with 100 soldiers guarding the tomb?"

After sundown prayers, the band of Jesus' followers dispersed in all directions. Lazarus and John returned to Jerusalem. Thomas, fearing it was too dangerous to remain in Jerusalem, decided to stay with his cousin in Bethany. The women scattered to the homes of several friends to collect the necessary oils and spices for treating Jesus' body. While none of them had resolved how they would get past the Roman guards or move the massive stone, they planned to return to the tomb at first light and complete their task, and bid their final farewell to their Jesus.

None of the women slept that night. The shock of Jesus' murder and the disturbing events of the day kept them all unsettled, confused, and afraid. Martha knew from the sound of the other women's breathing that everyone was awake. So with two hours left before daybreak she arose and lit the oil lamp. "We might as well go now as later," she announced to her guests. "The earlier we arrive, the less attention we will attract from His enemies."

As Martha's eyes adjusted to the lamplight, she looked about the room. "Where's Mary?" Finding the long night hours unbearable, Martha's younger sister had quietly slipped out into the darkness. Drawn by immeasurable love and ignoring her fears, Mary made her way to the tomb, alone.

It was still dark when the other women began their journey to Jerusalem. Pressing closely together to avoid stumbling on the narrow road, they recounted Christ's works of mercy and His words of comfort.

As they neared the place of His burial, they came upon a lone figure—Mary the wife of Clopas. She had traversed the seven miles from Emmaus alone to help them. Following a subdued greeting, Clopas' wife echoed the other women's nagging question: "Who is going to roll away the stone for us?"

Before anyone could respond, a brilliant white flash of lightning came from the cloudless predawn sky. It struck in the vicinity of the garden tomb. For an instant, all was as bright as noon, leaving the women momentarily blinded. The earth beneath their feet trembled and rolled. The mother of Jesus grabbed hold of Martha to keep from losing her balance. Martha spilled some of the spices and oil she was carrying as the bewildered women helplessly clung to one another.

As quickly as the earthquake began it subsided. Up ahead they heard frantic shouts and screams in the Latin tongue. They stared in surprise as a large band of men scrambled up the road to Jerusalem. As they ran, some of them staggered and fell as if they were drunk. The faint glimmer of armor in the early-morning light indicated that the fleeing men must be Roman soldiers.

The women stood transfixed, watching the spectacle.

"Something wonderful has happened," Jesus' mother whispered. After a few moments of ominous silence, the women silently proceeded in the direction of the Master's tomb.

Mary Magdalene arrived at the tomb moments after the flash of light and the earthquake. She cautiously moved into the garden clearing and discovered that the stone had been rolled away. Her first thought was that the guards had removed Jesus' body. Distressed at the thought of losing even the remains of her most precious Friend, she rushed to the open grave and guardedly peered inside. An unearthly light seemed to be illuminating the place where Jesus had lain. But the tomb was empty; His body was not there.

In anguish and shock, Mary stared in silence at the vacant ledge, barely breathing. Then she stepped out of the tomb and glanced about, dazed and astonished.

I must find the disciples, she thought. *They'll know what to do.* The grieving woman turned and hurried up the path the short distance to Herod's Gate and into Jerusalem. When she arrived at the house of John Mark, she found Peter and John awake and talking quietly on the roof patio.

Mary scampered up the stairs and gasped, "They have taken the Lord from the tomb, and we do not know where they have laid Him!" Although Mary hadn't meant to startle them, the edgy disciples jumped at the sound of her voice.

Peter was the first to recover. "What did you say?" he demanded.

Mary tried to catch her breath between her words. "I've been to the tomb. His body is gone. The stone is rolled away. The soldiers are gone too!"

John glanced toward Peter. "Who would do this?" he wondered.

"I don't know," Peter replied, "but we should go see for ourselves what has happened."

"Should we wake the others?" John asked.

"No," Peter answered. "This may be a trap the leaders are using to eliminate the rest of us. In fact, I will go alone. It could be dangerous."

"As God lives," John vowed, "I will go with you!"

As the men quietly rushed down the stairs and up to the city gates, they noted that the Roman guards were not at their post. As soon as he cleared the gate, young John broke into a full run and Peter struggled to keep up with him.

Without waiting for permission, Mary decided to follow them. She felt strangely drawn to the place where she had last seen her Jesus. She was determined to discover what had become of His body.

Martha and the other women entered the clearing and found Roman swords, helmets, and shields scattered about the area where Jesus had been buried. Mary, Clopas' wife, gasped and pointed. They were all startled by a tall stranger wearing a long white robe who sat upon the cracked stone that had covered the mouth of Jesus' grave. The huge stone had been rolled far away from the entrance and broken, as though Samson had flung it aside in anger.

The kind-looking man on the stone offered a reassuring smile to the frightened women. Recognizing their fear, he said, "Do not be afraid, for I know that you seek Jesus who was crucified. He is not here; for He is risen, as He said" (Matt. 28:5, 6). The stranger gracefully gestured with his hand toward the chamber in the hillside. "Come, see the place where the Lord lay" (verse 6).

The tall messenger smoothly slipped off the stone and walked toward the tomb. "Look for yourselves," he said cheerfully, motioning toward the entrance.

Jesus' mother stared at the face of this noble being. Then he smiled, and she recognized him as the angel Gabriel, who had announced Jesus' birth 34 years earlier.

As the bewildered women tried to digest the perplexing turn of events, the mother of Jesus moved cautiously toward the tomb's entrance. The other women timidly followed. Though frightened, step by step they moved, with a resolve born of love for their Lord. The unearthly light still glowed within the tomb. Inside, they saw another being sitting on the ledge where they had placed Jesus' body Friday evening. This stranger said, "Why do you seek the living among the dead? He is not here, but is risen! Remember how He spoke to you when He was still in Galilee, saying, 'The Son of man must be delivered into the hands of sinful men, and be crucified, and the third day rise again'" (Luke 24:5-7).

The stunned women backed out of the rock-hewn tomb. In a

whisper Martha repeated the words of the angel, at first as a question, "He is risen? He is risen?" Then she said it as a fact, "He is risen!" Then Martha did something completely out of character—she tossed aside the bag of embalming spices and ran as fast as she could toward Jerusalem. The other women followed close behind.

They had scarcely started up the narrow trail when they nearly collided with John, Peter, and then Mary Magdalene. Excited and almost hysterical with joy and confusion, the women, all at once, tried to tell them what they had seen and heard.

The astonishment on their faces told Peter something amazing had happened. "Go and tell the others in the city what you have seen!" he commanded.

Before Peter finished speaking, John bolted toward the tomb to see firsthand what had happened. He stopped in the clearing and surveyed the abandoned armaments from the Roman guard, then looked at the massive stone. John thought, *What terrific force could move it so far?* But the messengers the women spoke of appeared to be gone.

Panting and out of breath, Peter and Mary came up behind him. "Could the earthquake have done this?" John queried.

"No!" Peter shook his head resolutely. "An earthquake could never do that."

John walked to the tomb and peered inside. Peter didn't even pause, but boldly strode inside. The tomb was empty except for the two articles of neatly folded burial cloth. With trembling fingers John touched the linen. "It must be true!"

Peter nodded. "Only Jesus would take the time to fold these. But where is He?"

"I don't know." John glanced about nervously. "But we'd better leave. The soldiers might return and blame us for breaking Pilate's seal and stealing Jesus' body."

The two disciples emerged from the tomb to the first rays of the morning sun that were already gilding the walls of Jerusalem. Mary stood motionless and dazed, hugging herself against the spring morning chill.

"We must go, Mary." John gently touched her arm. "The guard may return."

Mary nodded, but remained transfixed by the confusing scene before her as Peter and John hurried up the trail. Regardless of the danger, she could not bring herself to leave the place. She had an overwhelming consciousness that Jesus was not far away.

Desperately hoping to find her Lord where she last saw Him, she walked slowly once again to the rock chamber. With one hand on the stone wall, she stooped and looked inside.

Suddenly she gasped at the sight before her eyes. Two men wearing glowing white garments stood inside. As Mary gazed speechless, one of the strangers asked, "Woman, why are you weeping?" (John 20:13).

An anguished sob escaped her lips. "Because they have taken away my Lord, and I do not know where they have laid Him" (verse 13).

Hoping to find someone to point her in the direction of Jesus, Mary turned from the two unusual men and backed out of the shallow cavern. She was overwhelmed with fear and confusion.

A part of her longed to run from the place, but something held her. Weeping uncontrollably, her heart heaving with grief, Mary staggered from the entrance of the tomb over to the broken stone that had covered the mouth of the cave an hour earlier. As she wept, she glanced toward the ground and spied the torn remains of the wax and string seal that Pilate had had placed on the stone. She remembered the story she had heard as a child of how King Darius had placed a similar seal on the stone cover when Daniel had been thrown into the lions' den. When that seal was broken, Daniel had come out alive.

While she was staring at the seal and pondering these thoughts, a long shadow passed between her and the morning sun. Startled by the silent approach of a stranger, Mary quickly glanced up.

The eastern sky shone bright from directly behind the dark silhouette of a Man, making it difficult for Mary to see His face. The Man gently asked, "Woman, why are you weeping? Whom are you looking for?"

Mary, assuming He was the gardener coming to begin his day's work, wondered, *How does he know I am looking for anyone?*

Realizing only the very rich could afford to be buried in a stone tomb such as this, and thinking possibly the rulers had evicted Jesus' body, Mary thought this man might know what had become of her Lord's remains.

"Sir, if You have carried Him away, tell me where You have laid Him, and I will take Him away" (John 20:15), the woman pleaded, dropping her head and turning to hide a fresh flow of tears.

Moved by her devotion, the kind Stranger could not bear to see her grieve another moment. He uttered the one word that would turn her sorrow into ecstasy.

"Mary!"

Suddenly a wave of joyful recognition swept through her. At the familiar, melodious sound of her name coming from the compassionate lips of Jesus, Mary whirled about and threw herself at His nail-scarred feet. "Rabboni! You're alive! You're alive!" She wept, clinging to His ankles and drenching His feet with her fresh tears of joy.

Kneeling beside her, He placed His hand on her head in blessing. With His other hand He gently dabbed away her tears with the sleeve of His shimmering robe. To Mary it felt as if He were caressing her tears away with a warm light.

Then Jesus said to her, "You must not detain Me, for I have not yet ascended to My Father. But go to My brethren and tell them, 'I am ascending to My Father and your Father, and to My God and your God.'"

After Jesus spoke these words, He stood up. As Mary reluctantly released her hold on His feet she beheld the most wonderful transformation. Jesus' face shone as bright as the morning sun. It was as if someone had peeled a veil from her eyes. She saw an innumerable company of beaming angels surrounding Him, and He began to rise up through this living corridor of indiscernible glory.

The angels sang a beautiful triumphant song: "Lift up your heads, O you gates! And be lifted up, you everlasting doors! And the King of glory shall come in" (Ps. 24:7). The unique strains of music were infinitely more wonderful than anything she had ever heard.

Before Jesus disappeared in the living cloud of angels, He turned toward Mary. She heard His voice echo down, saying, "I will never leave you."

Just as Mary thought she could not survive another moment of such incredible divine glory, it all vanished. By comparison, the freshly risen sun seemed dark. As Mary digested the magnitude of these events, she began to move up the trail toward Jerusalem. A new light burned in her mind, and energy animated her steps. The angelic music was silent, but Mary's heart was singing. "Jesus is alive! He is alive!" Then Mary paused on the trail to allow a most profound revelation to digest. "He waited for me? Yes, He chose me to tell the good news." As she continued up the trail she kept repeating, "Even me!"

All her life Mary had felt she was never good enough. Simon did not even think she was good enough to touch, let alone to wash, Jesus' feet. The religious leaders thought she was good enough only for stoning. But Jesus had waited until Peter, John, and even His own mother had left the tomb in order to commission her, a woman once considered a social outcast. The Saviour saw her as a new and clean vessel. He chose her to tell the world that He, the living God, her Friend and Saviour, had risen.

The Study

JOHN 20:11-18

"But Mary stood outside by the tomb weeping, and as she wept she stooped down and looked into the tomb. And she saw two angels in white sitting, one at the head and the other at the feet, where the body of Jesus had lain. Then they said to her, 'Woman, why are you weeping?' She said to them, 'Because they have taken away my Lord, and I do not know where they have laid Him.' Now when she had said this, she turned around and saw Jesus standing there, and did not know that it was Jesus. Jesus said to her, 'Woman, why are you weeping? Whom are you seeking?' She, supposing Him to be the gardener, said to Him, 'Sir, if You have carried Him away, tell me where You have laid Him, and I will take Him away.' Jesus said to her, 'Mary!' She turned and said to Him, 'Rabboni!' (which is to say, Teacher). Jesus said to her, 'Do not cling to Me, for I have not yet ascended to My Father; but go to My brethren and say to them, "I am ascending to My Father and your Father, and to My God and your God."' Mary Magdalene came and told the disciples that she had seen the Lord, and that He had spoken these things to her."

MARK 16:9-11

"Now when He rose early on the first day of the week, He appeared first to Mary Magdalene, out of whom He had cast seven demons. She went and told those who had been with Him, as they mourned and wept. And when they heard that He was alive and had been seen by her, they did not believe."

HE SHOOK THINGS UP

Thomas Jefferson was a great man, but alas, he was a deist and could not accept the miraculous elements in Scripture. He edited his own special version of the Bible in which all references to the supernatural were deleted. In editing the Gospels, Jefferson confined himself solely to the moral teachings of Jesus. The closing words of Jefferson's Bible are these: "There laid they Jesus and rolled a great stone at the mouth of the sepulchre and departed." Thank God, that is not the way the story really ends.

The resurrection of Jesus was verified by a mass of undeniable evidence. Not among the least of these proofs was the testimony of nature in the dark sky above and the shaking earth below. When Jesus came forth from the grave, there transpired a miniature sample of what will happen when He emerges in glory from the heavens to gather His children. Regarding these signs in the heavens and earth, Ellen G. White wrote: "An earthquake marked the hour when Christ laid down His life, and another earthquake witnessed the moment when He took up His life in triumph. He who had vanquished death and the grave came forth from the tomb with the tread of a conqueror, amid the reeling of the earth, the flashing of lightning, and the roaring of thunder. When He shall come to the earth again, He will shake 'not the earth only, but also heaven.' 'The earth shall reel to and fro like a drunkard, and shall be removed like a cottage.' 'The heavens shall be rolled together as a scroll;' 'the elements shall melt with fervent heat, the earth also and the works that are therein shall be burned up.' But 'the Lord will be the hope of His people, and the strength of the children of Israel' (Heb. 12:26; Isa. 24:20; 34:4; 2 Peter 3:10; Joel 3:16)" (*The Desire of Ages*, p. 780).

Living in California, I have experienced a few earthquakes. It can be very unnerving when the ground under your feet begins to sway and roll. We go through life thinking we can trust the ground to be constant and dependable. If nothing else, earthquakes have taught me that the only thing that cannot be moved is that which is rooted in God. "Heaven and earth will pass away, but My words will by no means pass away" (Matt. 24:35).

THREE DAYS AND THREE NIGHTS?

So, how long was Jesus in the tomb, and does it matter?

"Then some of the scribes and Pharisees answered, saying, 'Teacher, we want to see a sign from You.' But he answered and said unto them, 'An evil and adulterous generation seeks after a sign, no sign will be given to it except the sign of the prophet Jonah. For as Jonah was three days and three nights in the belly of the great fish, so will the Son of Man be three days and three nights in the heart of the earth'" (Matt. 12:38–40).

Many people have been confounded by the above scripture because Jesus clearly said, "The Son of Man will be three days and three nights in the heart of the earth." Assuming that "in the heart of the earth" means in the tomb, and if Jesus died Friday and rose Sunday, He was not in the tomb three nights. One way to understand this passage is to realize that "heart of the earth" does not mean the tomb. "Heart of the earth" can easily be translated "in the midst of the world" or in the grip of this lost planet that Jesus came to save.

The phrase "in the earth" appears dozens of times in the King James Version. Not one of those references is to the grave. Take, for example, the phrase in the Lord's Prayer, "Thy will be done in earth as it is in heaven." Does that mean for God's will to be done in the tomb or the grave, as it is in heaven? No, of course not! It means that it be done among the people of earth—the nations of the earth—as it is done among the angels in heaven.

Jesus' suffering for the sins of the world did not begin on the cross on Friday. He began suffering for our sins right after He ate the Last Supper. Several times Jesus said that "the hour has come," referring to that Thursday night (Matt. 26:45; Mark 14:41; Luke 22:14; John 16:32; John 17:1). Jesus' ordeal began when the mob arrested Him Thursday night. "In the heart of the earth" really means "in the grip of the world." (Remember, Satan is called the prince of this world in John 12:31.) For three days and three nights Jesus was separated from the Father's protection and was in the hands of the enemy. He was a captive "in the heart of the earth" as He suffered the penalty and punishment for the sins of the world.

WHERE DID HE GO?

Many other people struggle with the issue of where Jesus went when He died on the cross. Most of the confusion again springs from the misinterpretation of one passage of Scripture.

"For Christ also hath once suffered for sins, the just for the unjust, that he might bring us to God, being put to death in the flesh, but quickened by the Spirit: by which also he went and preached unto the spirits in prison; which sometime were disobedient, when once the longsuffering of God waited in the days of Noah, while the ark was a preparing, wherein few, that is, eight souls were saved by water" (1 Peter 3:18-20, KJV).

At first glance many have thought that this means that Jesus was not really dead on the cross but that instead He was transported to some spirit realm. There, it is believed by some, He preached to the spirits of the people who lived before the Flood, to give them a second chance at salvation. This teaching is echoed in the Apostles' Creed. But many do not realize that the Apostles' Creed was not written by the apostles at all; it was written about 100 years after the last of the apostles had died. It is no part of inspired Scripture.

This theory is the antithesis of every Bible teaching on the subject. The Scriptures are clear that after death there are no second chances for conversion: "It is appointed for men to die once, but after this the judgment" (Heb. 9:27). "For we must all appear before the judgment seat of Christ, that each one may receive the things done in the body, according to what he has done, whether good or bad" (2 Cor. 5:10).

Look carefully at 1 Peter 4:6. It says that the gospel was preached to "them that *are* dead" (KJV). They are dead now, but they were not dead when the gospel was preached to them. It would be a very difficult thing to preach to dead people. It's hard enough to preach to those who are alive. It takes intelligence and knowledge to understand the gospel, and such intelligence is possessed only by those who are alive (Eccl. 9:5, 10).

Peter says, "By which [Spirit] also he went and preached unto the spirits in prison" (1 Peter 3:19, KJV). By the same Spirit that eventually raised Jesus, at the time of the Flood Jesus (God) preached to the people who were then alive, imprisoned by sin. Compare this with the famous statement in Genesis 6:3: "My Spirit shall not strive with man forever, for he is indeed flesh; yet his days shall be one hundred and twenty years."

"But if the Spirit of Him who raised Jesus from the dead dwells in you, He who raised Christ from the dead will also give life to your mortal bodies through His Spirit who dwells in you" (Rom. 8:11).

So you can see that Peter is not saying that when Jesus died He went to some mystical dungeon to preach to the spirits of people who lived before the Flood. Rather, he is saying it was the same Holy Spirit that preached to them, who resurrected Jesus and also preaches to us.

Still others struggle with the very thought that Jesus, God the Son, died! They wonder, "How could God die?" I don't know! But I also cannot explain how God could become a man! The Bible describes this as a mystery: "And without controversy great is the mystery of godliness: God was manifested in the flesh" (1 Tim. 3:16). But it is very dangerous to tamper with the plain teachings of Scripture. The penalty for sin is death (Rom. 6:23). If Jesus did not really die on the cross but was simply transported into some other spiritual dimension, we are undermining one of the foundational truths of the gospel. The Bible clearly says that Jesus died (Rom. 5:6; 1 Cor. 15:3), and we must accept His word even if we cannot explain it all. That is called faith.

Love lingers

Near Greyfriars churchyard in Edinburgh, Scotland, is a memorial fountain and statue to a little dog named Greyfriars Bobby. In 1858 a man called Jock Grey was buried in the church cemetery. His faithful little dog mournfully watched at the spot where his old master had been committed to the grave. For the next 14 years, day and night, rain or shine, until his own death in 1872 the loyal canine virtually lived on top of his master's tomb. The little Skye terrier left the site for only an hour at a time to visit his two friends, the restaurateur who fed him and the sexton who built a shelter for him at the cemetery.

During his 14-year vigil, thousands visited the yard to see this faithful little dog. In tribute to his lifelong loyalty and devotion, they buried him in the church graveyard beside his master.

After everyone else had left Jesus' garden tomb, Mary loyally lingered where she had last seen her Lord. Sometimes we lose track of Jesus because we become preoccupied with our own will and agendas. We become distracted with earthly relationships and forget our heavenly Friend.

Even Jesus' own mother and father lost track of their treasured trust after they visited the Temple in Jerusalem. But they found Jesus three days later, right where they had last seen Him. Mary said, "Behold, thy father and I have sought thee sorrowing" (Luke 2:48, KJV). When we carelessly lose track of our Master we might have to spend some time searching and sorrowing to find Him again. Just like Jesus' mother, Mary Magdalene found Jesus three days later by lingering where she had last seen her Master.

"Love suffers long and is kind; love does not envy; love does not parade itself, is not puffed up; does not behave rudely, does not seek its own, is not provoked, thinks no evil; does not rejoice in iniquity, but rejoices in the truth; bears all things, believes all things, hopes all things, endures all things. Love never fails" (1 Cor. 13:4-8).

KNOWING HE IS NEAR

"That they should seek the Lord, if haply they might feel after him, and find him, though he be not far from every one of us" (Acts 17:27).

During the preliminaries at one of his large crusades, Billy Graham donned a cap and sunglasses and walked around incognito to gather objective feedback from his audience. Seeing an indifferent-looking visitor leaning against the stadium gate, Graham asked him, "Don't you want to go in? The meetings have started!"

"Naw," the man drawled, "I don't care much for the warm-up act. I'm here to see the big gun!" Little did he know that he was talking to the "big gun." In like manner, we miss many blessings because we do not know when Jesus is near. Jesus said to the Samaritan woman at the well, "If you knew the gift of God, and who it is who says to you, 'Give Me a drink,' you would have asked Him, and He would have given you living water" (John 4:10).

Knowing the Lord is near brings us joy. In our story Mary was weeping because she did not know it was the Lord standing beside her. "Now when she had said this, she turned around and saw Jesus standing there, and did not know that it was Jesus" (John 20:14). When later that day Jesus appeared to two of the disciples on the road to Emmaus, they also were sad because they did not know who walked with them. "They did not know Him. And He said to them,

'What kind of conversation is this that you have with one another as you walk and are sad?'" (Luke 24:16, 17).

How many the world over walk through life sad and disconso late because they do not know or believe that Jesus is near. A newly converted Chinese American named Lo Chang began to shout for joy when he read the end of the Gospel of Matthew as recorded in the King James Version: "And, lo, I am with you alway, even unto the end of the world" (Matt. 28:20). Lo was especially happy because he took the promise personally—"Lo [his name], I am with you." How many professed Christians suffer needless sorrow simply because we forget the promise of Jesus' presence. They do not know that Jesus is near to help them bear their burdens. "Casting all your care upon Him, for He cares for you" (1 Peter 5:7).

ADOPTED INTO THE FAMILY

A Sunday school teacher had to register two new boys in Sunday school. When she asked their birthdays the bolder of the two said, "We're both 7. My birthday is April 8, 1976, and my brother's is April 20, 1976."

"But that's impossible!" answered the teacher.

"No, it's not," answered the other brother. "One of us is adopted."

"Which one?" asked the teacher.

The boys looked at each other and smiled. The first boy said, "We asked Dad awhile ago, but he said he loved us both, and just couldn't remember which one was adopted."

The last words Jesus spoke to Mary confirmed that she had been completely embraced as a daughter of God: "Go to My brethren and say to them, 'I am ascending to My Father and your Father, and to My God and your God'" (John 20:17). She had been fully accepted and adopted into God's family as surely as Mordecai had adopted Esther, and as surely as Rahab the harlot had become a mother in Israel. "You received the Spirit of adoption by whom we cry out, 'Abba, Father'" (Rom. 8:15). "I will be a Father to you, and you shall be My sons and daughters, says the Lord Almighty" (2 Cor. 6:18).

Holding the Gardener's heel

"Jesus said to her, 'Woman, why are you weeping? Whom are you seeking?' She, supposing Him to be the gardener, said to Him, 'Sir, if You have carried Him away, tell me where You have laid Him, and I will take Him away'" (John 20:15).

This is the only time the word "gardener" is found in the Bible. Interestingly enough, it is applied to Jesus. Mary was right—Jesus was the Gardener. The Bible teaches, "The Lord God planted a garden eastward in Eden" (Gen. 2:8). Furthermore, the Lord still gardens today. The seed is the Word of God, and we are His plants. "For the vineyard of the Lord of hosts is the house of Israel, and the men of Judah are His pleasant plant" (Isa. 5:7).

In that first garden the Lord pronounced a prophecy to the first woman: "And I will put enmity between you and the woman, and between your seed and her Seed; He shall bruise your head, and you shall bruise His heel" (Gen. 3:15).

Jesus was the Seed of the woman, who would crush the head of the serpent. But it was not without cost. He would have His heel bruised. When Jesus triumphed over death and Satan, He still bore in His feet the scars from the cross. And Mary, like the church today, must fall at His scarred and bruised heel to worship.

We come to go

Not only did Jesus save Mary; He gave her a job to do. Everyone whom the Lord cleans He commissions. After Isaiah had his lips cleaned with a coal from God's altar, the Lord commissioned him to go and preach (Isa. 6:1-9).

Basically, Jesus said to Mary, "Don't just cling to Me; go and tell others." If we love Jesus as Mary loved Jesus, we are compelled to tell others. We can't keep Him to ourselves. The man from whom Jesus purged an army of demons wanted to just stay at His side. "Now the man from whom the demons had departed begged Him that he might be with Him. But Jesus sent him away, saying, 'Return to your own house, and tell what great things God has done for you'" (Luke 8:38, 39). Like Mary and this man, the church is saved for the purpose of telling others.

Salvation involves coming and going. We come to Jesus at His great invitation, then we go for Jesus with the Great Commission. "Come to Me, all you who labor and are heavy laden, and I will give you rest" (Matt. 11:28). "Go therefore and make disciples of all the nations" (Matt. 28:19). "Now therefore come, that we may go and tell the king's household" (2 Kings 7:9, KJV).

We should not go for Jesus until we first come to Jesus.

God uses people to reach people. He could preach the gospel much more efficiently through angels. However, witnessing is part of our sanctification process. Mary is never identified as having an exceptional gift of communication, but the Lord chose her to communicate the good news of His resurrection. This should encourage each of us to come to Jesus that we might go for Jesus and become witnesses of His resurrection.

A FORMULA AND PATTERN FOR SPIRITUAL SUCCESS

It is interesting to note that in the Gospels there is no record that a woman ever did anything to hurt Jesus. Men schemed against, spied on, spit on, and smote Jesus, but we never see a woman harming Jesus in any way during His earthly life. You remember from our earlier studies that among Bible symbols a woman represents a church. In summary, notice how Mary's life and story is a pattern for revival and vitality for God's people collectively, and for each of us as individuals.

1. Like Mary, we must spend time at Jesus' feet, crying tears of repentance for our sins as Mary did in the Temple. Then we hear Jesus declare that He does not condemn us. "Go and sin no more," He says to us.

2. As Mary did for Lazarus, each Christian needs to spend time at Jesus' feet, pleading and praying for friends and family who are spiritually dead, that He will give them life.

3. Like Mary, God's people need to make quality time for reading and hearing the Word at Jesus' feet. Mary is recorded in Scripture as saying very little; apparently she spent more time listening than talking.

4. Like Mary, the church will thrive only when she understands the commitment and beauty of sacrificial giving.

5. It is crucial that we spend much time at Jesus' feet, beholding Him on the cross for our sins. It is here that we have our love batteries recharged.

6. Mary spent time serving Jesus, both at Simon's feast and when she helped with His burial. Likewise, we will want to serve Him after seeing how much He loves us.

7. Finally, to proclaim the living Saviour joyfully to others is the privilege and responsibility of every child of God.

IT'S HARD TO HIDE GOOD NEWS

Lawrence Maxwell tells the story of a group of prospectors who set out from Bannack, Montana (then capital of the state), in search of gold. They endured many hardships. Several of their company died enroute. They were overtaken by Indians who took their good horses, leaving them with only a few aging ponies.

Then their attackers threatened them, telling them to get back to Bannack and stay there. The Indians declared, "If we find you out here again, we'll murder the lot of you."

Defeated, discouraged, and depressed, the prospectors made their way back toward the capital city. At one point, as they tethered out the exhausted ponies along the side of a creek, one of the men casually picked up a small stone from the creekbed.

He called to his buddy, "Got a hammer?" Upon cracking the rock, the miner said, "It looks as though there may be gold here."

The two of them panned for gold the rest of the afternoon and managed to collect $12 worth. The next day the entire company panned for gold in the creek. They found $50 worth, a great sum in those days.

"We have struck it!" they said to each other. The men made their way back to Bannack, vowing not to breathe a single word concerning their gold strike. They discreetly reequipped themselves with supplies for another prospecting trip. But when they set out of town, 300 men followed them. Who had divulged their secret? No one! Their beaming faces betrayed their treasure!

Like the prospectors and their good fortune, if we become enamored with Jesus, if we truly comprehend the good news of the gospel, we cannot conceal the joy of our discovery. Our beaming faces will betray our secret.

The last image we see of Mary in the Sacred Record is that of a fleeting form with a shining face. She is running on air because she has burning in her heart the most wonderful news the world has ever heard. Her voice is heard singing hosannas as she races up the road to Jerusalem to tell the world, "He is alive!"

EMPTY AND BROKEN

When Thomas Edison was working on the incandescent light-bulb, he found that even the best filament would burn out in an instant unless he placed it in a vacuum. Robbed of oxygen, the right element continued to burn for many hours. Likewise, the light of Jesus cannot burn in a heart that is full of other things. The oil of God's Spirit can be poured only into empty vessels (2 Kings 4:3).

Vance Havner tells us, "God uses broken things. It takes broken soil to produce a crop; broken clouds to give rain; broken grain to give bread; broken bread to give strength. It is the broken alabaster box that gives forth perfume—it is Peter, weeping bitterly, who returns to greater power than ever."

Jesus could use Mary for great things because through trials her soul had been vacuumed of self and was yearning for His filling. She had made a complete surrender while passing through the superheated crucible of repentance.

THE LAST SHALL BE FIRST

"Now when He rose early on the first day of the week, He appeared first to Mary Magdalene, out of whom He had cast seven demons" (Mark 16:9).

I would never have orchestrated the Resurrection the way the Lord chose to do it. After escaping the tomb I would have appeared to Herod or Pilate and gloated about how impotent were their soldiers, seal, and stone to prevent me from rising. I would have dared Herod to fetch the purple robe and crown of thorns if he had the audacity to mock me again. Or at least I would have appeared to the high priest and leaders who condemned me and made them squirm and shake in their sandals. I would have watched the blood drain from their faces as they pondered the terrible truth that they had condemned and executed their long-awaited Messiah. If I were producing the Resurrection, I would at least have Jesus initially appear to the disciples or perhaps to His mother, Mary.

But Jesus chose to pass by all these logical options; He first revealed Himself to a social outcast. Jesus deliberately waited until Peter, John, and even His own mother had left the garden area to bestow on a formerly demon-possessed prostitute, saved by grace, the highest honor ever to be granted any mortal. Why? Why is it that the first words spoken by Jesus after His resurrection were to Mary, and yet this is the last time she appears in the Sacred Record? To highlight and underscore the truth that He came to seek and save the lost. To remind us that if He can transform, save, and commission a meek and weak girl named Mary—well, then, there is hope for each one of us.

The Richest
CAVEMAN
The Doug Batchelor Story

This great witnessing book tells how God turned a rebellious teenager living in a cave into a tremendous soul-winner. This extraordinary true story of Doug Batchelor, son of millionaire and show-business mother, includes eight pages of pictures! This book is available in both English and Spanish.

US$7.95

MOUNTAIN MINISTRY
5431 Auburn Blvd., Suite A-1
Sacramento, CA 95841

How to Survive
and Thrive
in Church

No matter whether your church is big, small, dead, divided, scandal-torn, or gossip-ridden, you can learn not just how to survive, but also how to thrive and to be a blessing to others.

US$8.95

MOUNTAIN MINISTRY

5431 Auburn Blvd., Suite A-1
Sacramento, CA 95841

To See the King

Seven Steps to Salvation

By comparing his own true-life experiences with those described in Isaiah 6:1-8, Doug Batchelor shows that understanding and experiencing salvation are not at all difficult. A great book to share!

US$2.49

To place an order, call 916-332-5800 or write to Mountain Ministry, 5431 Auburn Blvd., Suite A-1, Sacramento, CA 95841. Or call your local ABC at 1-800-765-6955 (in the U.S.)

Prices subject to change without notice.

MOUNTAIN MINISTRY
5431 Auburn Blvd., Suite A-1
Sacramento, CA 95841